Big Projects
for Little Hands

Ages 3–8

Written by Jennifer Dorval

Illustrations by Kelly McMahon

 Teacher Created Materials

Teacher Created Materials, Inc.

6421 Industry Way

Westminster, CA 92683

www.teachercreated.com

©2002 Teacher Created Materials, Inc.

Made in U.S.A.

ISBN 0-7439-3201-3

Library of Congress Catalog Card Number: 2001 09 2263

Editor:

Polly Hoffman

Table of Contents

Table of Contents *(cont.)*

Introduction

Welcome to Big Projects for Little Hands!

This 160 page book is filled with exciting projects, done on a larger scale, for young children who already like to think big! Many of the projects can be used for fun and creative play after your child has created it. The activities are geared for children between the ages of three and eight, with varying levels of difficulty. Parents, however, may feel just as compelled to share in the happy hours of creating and playing.

Projects are set out as follows:

- **Materials:** This section lists everything you need to complete this project. Most materials should be easily found around the house or at craft, hardware, fabric, or your local grocery stores. If there is a material required that is somewhat unusual, a suggestion will be offered as to where to find it.

- **Preparation:** This section will be in projects where some parts of the craft are to be done by an adult in advance.

- **Let's Do It:** This section lays out the project in easy to follow, step-by-step instructions.

- **How to Play:** This section is in projects where a game is created and explains how to play the game.

- **More Ideas:** This section offers ways to adapt the activity to different age levels, vary or extend the project, or make it work on a smaller scale.

For your convenience the activities have been divided into four thrilling themes.

- **Fairy Tales and Nursery Rhymes:** Several marvelous crafts are included to extend a favorite tale or nursery rhyme. Projects are fantasy in general, with some designed for a specific fairy tale or nursery rhyme.

- **Insects and Spiders:** These are great activities for children who love the creepy and the crawly. These projects are great for anytime and would make great Halloween decorations.

- **Dinosaurs:** Dinosaurs fascinate many children because they were big and mighty and lived millions of years ago. This theme fits perfectly in *Big Projects for Little Hands*.

- **Animals:** This section contains a variety of projects centered around a variety of animals both wild and tame.

How to Use This Book

Previewing the Book: Browse through the pages of the book to familiarize yourself with the types of projects and the layout of the sections. Artwork showing some of the completed projects is included to help clarify the instructions.

Gathering Materials: Note the things that you can begin to collect and recycle as you go about your daily activities. These could include things found in the home, such as plastic bottles and jugs; different-sized cans; Styrofoam egg cartons and meat trays; and bits of fabric, ribbon and string. You may find things in nature such as feathers or rocks. There may be other items that you will want to purchase and keep on hand: craft sticks, construction paper, pipe cleaners, scissors, tacky glue, tape, paint and brushes, and markers and crayons.

Storing Materials: Set aside an area, such as a shelf or drawer, that will serve as a permanent place to store all craft materials. Make the storage place accessible to your children so they can contribute collectibles whenever they find something they think would be fun to use. Remind children to respect others and nature by asking before they take anything that is not theirs. Tell children to check with an adult before taking something from the environment.

Getting Started: Help children get started by reading the directions aloud together and talking about the project that has been chosen. Be sure to check the "Materials" section to ensure that you have the necessary items to complete the project. Older kids will probably be able to complete most crafts with only a little help. Younger children may need further assistance gathering materials and following the directions.

Safety Concerns: Remember to read the safety guidelines on page 7 before starting each art project to minimize the risk of accidents. Note the projects that will require your continued active involvement because of safety concerns or difficulty. Guide children to choose projects that are appropriate for the amount of time you have available.

Encouraging Creativity: You may be tempted to do things yourself, but be patient and remember that these are your children's creations. Contribute only what is necessary to proceed with the project. Enjoy this creative time with your children and have fun!

Safety Guidelines

For Adults:

- Remember to read the directions completely and carefully before you help your children start a project.
- Actively assist with the crafts that require adult supervision for safety—those that use an iron, hot glue gun, stove, sharp utensils or tools.
- Thoroughly clean all previously used containers. Add a little bleach to the cleaning water to kill bacteria.
- Never use meat trays that have held raw chicken. The butcher in your local grocery store will usually give out unused ones if you ask.
- Cover work surfaces with a protective layer of cloth, plastic, cardboard or newspaper.
- When working with younger children, be sure to hand out smaller items, such as seeds and buttons, one at a time. Be sure to stress that these items should never be put in their mouths.
- Model "safety first" behavior as you work with your children. When you are through using an implement, put it away, turn it off, or otherwise secure it to prevent injury.
- Teach children to clean up and put things away in their proper places after completing each project.

For Children:

Be sure to ask an adult for help when you need to use the following:

- sharp objects such as scissors, knives, pins, and needles.
- hot items such as irons, glue guns, ovens, and stoves.
- tools such as hammers, screwdrivers, and sewing machines.

Fairy Tales and Nursery Rhymes

8

Fairy Tales and Nursery Rhymes

Fun Books to Read and Web Sites to Explore:

Briggs, Raymond. **Jim and the Beanstalk.** Coward-McCann, Inc., 1989.

Eagle, Kin. **Hey Diddle Diddle.** Whispering Coyote Press, 1997.

Edwards, Pamela Duncan. **Dinorella: A Prehistoric Fairy Tale.** Scholastic Inc., 1998.

Goode, Diane. **Cinderella: The Dog and Her Glass.** The Blue Sky Press, 2000.

Jackson, Ellen. **Cinder Edna.** Mulberry Books, 1994.

Paulson, Tim. **Jack and the Beanstalk/the Beanstalk Incident (Upside Down Tales).** Carol Publishing Group, 1990.

Scieszka, Jon. **The Stinky Cheese Man and Other Fairly Stupid Tales.** Scholastic Inc., 1992.

Scieszka, Jon. **The True Story of the Three Little Pigs!** Scholastic Inc., 1989.

Shorto, Russell. **Cinderella/the Untold Story of Cinderella (Upside Down Tales).** Carol Publishing Group, 1992.

Thaler, Mike. **Cinderella Bigfoot (Happily Ever Laughter).** Scholastic Inc., 1997.

Thaler, Mike. **Schmoe White and the Seven Dorfs (Happily Ever Laughter).** Scholastic Inc., 1997.

Trapani, Iza. **Oh Where, Oh Where Has My Little Dog Gone?** Whispering Coyote Press, 1994.

Trapani, Iza. **Twinkle, Twinkle, Little Star.** Whispering Coyote Press, 1994.

Web Sites:

Giggle Poetry
www.gigglepoetry.com

Mama Lisa's House of Nursery Rhymes
www.mamalisa.com/house/

Rebus Rhymes—Mother Goose and Others
www.EnchantedLearning.com/Rhymes.html

Castle Boxes

10

Castle Boxes

Materials

- Boxes of all sizes (from refrigerator to cereal)
- Double-sided adhesive tape
- Tempera paint and paintbrush
- Construction paper
- Scissors
- Large roll of newsprint paper or wrapping paper

Let's Do It

a. Cover the boxes in newsprint paper using the double-sided tape, so boxes can easily be painted over.

b. Stack and overlap boxes to construct a castle formation. Place the smaller boxes on top to make pillars, using the larger boxes as the foundation. Leave an opening to walk through. (Depending on the amount of boxes you have, you may want to construct the inside walls as well, or just the front of the castle.)

c. Cut out cones for the roof of the castle using construction paper.

d. Paint the entire structure with tempera paint and allow it to dry.

e. Decorate the walls by painting windows and vines.

More Ideas

Use string, and a large piece of cardboard, to create a drawbridge door for your castle. Poke a hole in each side of the castle and insert the string. Be sure to leave enough slack so that the door can be opened and closed without breaking.

Paint the castle a brownish red and then add black lines to create a brick or rock design.

Princess Nylon

12

Princess Nylon

Materials

- Three pairs of old panty hose
- Long flowing gown and old shoes
- Poster board
- Star stickers
- Acrylic paint and paintbrush
- Yellow or brown yarn
- Three 1" (2.5 cm) wide strips of tissue paper
- Newspaper and plain white paper
- Packing or masking tape
- Wire coat hanger or thick wire
- Wire cutters
- One rubber band
- Scissors

Let's Do It

a. Crumple up newspaper and stuff the legs of two pairs of panty hose, making the legs of one pair longer than the other pair.

b. Use the longer pair of nylons for the legs of the princess and the shorter pair for the arms, using the waist sections of each pair to make a body.

c. Using the wire cutters, cut a 10" (25 cm) piece of wire and place the wire in the middle of the waist sections to join the two pairs of nylons together, taping the waist sections together to make the body.

d. Crumple white paper and stuff one foot of the third pair of nylons to make a facial shape. Cut the rest of the nylons off and secure the stuffed nylon face with a rubber band.

e. Cut a 5" (12.5 cm) piece of wire and stick part of the wire into the bottom of the face and the other part of the wire into the top of the body to connect everything together.

f. Dress the princess in a long flowing gown and place shoes on her feet.

g. Use the acrylic paint and a paintbrush to paint a face on the princess.

h. Roll the poster board into a cone shape and tape it together to make a hat.

i. Decorate the hat with stars and strips of tissue paper taped to the top of the hat. Tape the pieces of yarn around the inside edges of the hat to make hair.

j. Attach the hat to the princess with tape or glue.

More Ideas

Make a nylon knight by making the body the same, but wrap the body in tin foil to represent armor.

Jungle Book Boxes

Jungle Book Boxes

Materials

- Medium-sized box
- Green and brown tempera paint and paintbrush
- Thick rope or yarn
- Green construction paper
- Two toilet paper rolls
- Tape
- Colored play dough
- Scissors
- Plastic plant stems
- Mini animal figurines
- Styrofoam meat tray
- Blue hair gel
- Stapler and staples

Let's Do It

a. Paint the inside and outside of the box green and allow it to dry completely. Place the box on its side, so the opening of the box is to the front.

b. Cut leaves out of green construction paper and staple them to the thick rope or yarn, to make leafy vines. Attach the vines with tape inside the box top at the top and let them dangle down.

c. Paint the toilet paper rolls brown and allow them to dry. Cut two 1" (2.5 cm) slits down the sides of the toilet paper rolls. Insert green leaves, cut from green construction paper, in the slits.

d. Place the toilet paper roll trees inside the box.

e. Use play dough to make snakes and other jungle creatures and place them in the box.

f. Decorate the inside with plastic plant stems to make the jungle look a little more realistic.

g. Use the Styrofoam meat tray as a container for a small river or stream in the jungle by putting the blue hair gel in it and placing it on the ground of the jungle box.

h. Miniature plastic animals add wonderful decoration to this newly created jungle.

More Ideas

Make Little Mermaid Scenes by painting the boxes completely blue instead of green. Decorate the inside with stuffed paper fish and a garbage bag octopus. See page 141 for instructions.

Do this same project on a smaller scale by using a shoe box.

Mirror, Mirror

16

Mirror, Mirror

Materials

- Large bubble mailer
- Tin foil
- Your favorite photos of yourself, your pets and/or your family
- One large paper clip, unfolded
- Hot glue gun and glue stick
- Double-sided adhesive tape
- Gold glitter glue
- Scissors

Let's Do It

a. Cut the bubble mailer into a large oval shape.

b. Cover the shaped mailer with tin foil, so that one side is completely covered.

c. The side that isn't completely covered will be the back. Put small drops of glue around the edges to hold the tin foil in place.

d. While the glue gun is warm, place a paper clip towards the top at the back and glue the bottom half of the clip onto the tinfoil mailer. This can be used to hang the mirror up.

e. Crop your favorite pictures and arrange them on the mirror. Use double-sided tape to attach the pictures to the mirror.

f. Decorate around the pictures on the mirror with gold glitter glue to help the pictures stand out.

g. Hang your new vanity mirror for all to see, and be proud of yourself.

More Ideas

If you would like to be able to change the pictures monthly or weekly, use a small amount of sticky tack (reusable adhesive) to hold pictures in place instead of the double-sided tape.

Use tin foil as a matte in a picture frame by covering the cardboard background with tin foil and centering a smaller picture in the middle. Put the cardboard background back in the picture frame and enjoy a shiny new matte for your picture.

101 Spots on Pots

18

101 Spots on Pots

Materials

- Large white flowerpot or planter
- Pencil or black pencil crayon
- Black, red, and blue acrylic paint and paintbrush
- Plant and potting soil

Let's Do It

a. Determine which side of the pot will be used for the face of your Dalmatian puppy pot. With a pencil, draw the face of the puppy on your pot. You can erase it until you are happy with it.

b. After you have drawn a face on the pot, begin painting it. Red can be used for the tongue and blue for the eyes, with black being the outlining color.

c. Draw spots around the whole pot, and draw a thick, red band around the bottom to represent the collar.

d. Paint the spots black.

e. Fill the planter with potting soil and plant your favorite plant inside.

More Ideas

Make a spotted garbage pail for your room by doing the same thing to a white garbage pail instead of using a white planter.

Make a spotted canister set by using four different-sized tin cans and painting them white with acrylic paint. Paint matching faces and spots on all of them. Fill with coffee, tea, sugar, and flour. This might be nice for a Mother's Day gift!

Fairy Tale Photo Book

Prince the magical dog got a job at the circus.

He became famous as "Prince the Fantastic Flying Dog."

Fairy Tale Photo Book

Materials

- Computer and printer
- Six photos on disk or CD
- Iron-on T-shirt transfer sheets
- Six 12" (80 cm) squares of white cotton material
- Stuffing or batting for inside
- Sewing machine or needle and white thread
- Iron and ironing board
- Ribbon and fabric glue

Let's Do It

a. Write a short fairy tale or story about the photos that you have.

b. Type part of your story above or below each of the pictures, using your favorite computer program to create your own six-page book.

c. Print the six pages onto iron-on T-shirt transfer sheets.

d. Follow the directions on your package of transfer sheets (as each kind is a little different).

e. Iron each transfer sheet onto the six squares of cotton material.

f. Place the cover page and the first page together with the pictures facing each other. Sew three of the sides together, leaving one side open.

g. Using the open side, turn the sewn edges to the inside, so that the pictures now face the front.

h. Fill the inside with stuffing and sew the fourth side together.

i. Repeat steps f, g, and h for pages two, three, four, and five.

j. Place the book in numerical order and sew the three pages together along the inside edge.

k. Cover the sewn edge by gluing ribbon along both sides.

l. Enjoy reading your new creation.

More Ideas

If a computer and printer is unavailable, place your pictures on white 8.5" x 11" paper and print your story underneath. Take your six sheets to a local color printer and have them copy your sheets onto the iron-on T-shirt transfers. Then, follow the directions from steps e-l for your book.

Puppet Theatre

22

Puppet Theatre

Materials

- An old refrigerator or hot water heater box
- Craft knife
- Staple gun and staples
- Tissue paper or paint
- Glue
- Old curtains or shower curtain
- Puppets

Adult Preparation

a. Cut out one whole side and the bottom of the box using the craft knife. Also, cut a window in the front of the box. The window should be as wide as the box, and stretch from the top of the box down almost half way.

b. Using the staple gun and staples, secure the top together tightly by stapling the top flaps together so the puppet stage doesn't collapse.

c. Along the inside top part of the roof, staple the curtain in place, so it hangs down just enough to cover the opening. If your curtain is too long, cut it to fit.

Let's Do It

a. Cut tissue paper and glue it to cover all of the outside showing cardboard. If you would rather, use a variety of colors of paint to decorate the puppet stage.

b. Use your favorite puppets or make your own to put on a puppet show.

More Ideas

Make a finger puppet theatre by cutting a rectangle opening in the bottom of a shoebox. Cover the outside in tissue paper and place a small piece of cloth or material on the inside to cover the window opening. Glue the material, inside at the top, so your finger puppets can peek through.

Use white athletic socks to make puppets. Use buttons for eyes and yarn for hair. If making an animal, use felt for ears and other specific features.

Cube Story Mix-up

Cube Story Mix-up

Materials

- Three large boxes of the same size
- Tempera paint and brush
- Double-sided tape
- Newsprint paper or wrapping paper
- Pencil

Let's Do It

a. Cover the boxes with paper, using the double-sided tape, so they will be easier to paint.

b. On one box, use a pencil to draw good characters from different stories on each of the six sides. For example, you might draw Cinderella and the Prince on one side, Snow White and the Seven Dwarfs on another side, the three little pigs, Jack, etc. to fill all six sides.

c. On the second box, use a pencil to draw the bad or evil characters from the same six stories—one per side, to fill all six sides.

d. With the last box, draw the settings for each of the six stories on the different sides to fill it.

e. Paint the pictures drawn on the boxes and allow time to dry.

f. Retell each story and then mix them up.

More Ideas

Roll the boxes like dice one at a time to create new funny stories with the results. For example, you may need to tell a story about Cinderella and the Prince climbing up a beanstalk to escape from the Big Bad Wolf.

Create silly stories by combining good characters, bad characters and story settings from different tales. Write them out and illustrate them.

Cool Princess Costume

Cool Princess Costume

Materials

- Handkerchief or scarf
- Star stickers
- Tin foil
- Scissors
- Glue
- Tape
- poster board (in your favorite color)
- Long dress
- String or yarn
- Hole punch

Let's Do It

a. Fold the poster board to form a cone-shaped hat by cutting the bottom to make it even. Tape the inside edges so they will stay together.

b. Place the handkerchief or scarf in the point at the top using tape to hold it in place.

c. Decorate the hat with star stickers.

d. Cut a 3" (7.5 cm) strip of tin foil that is long enough to fit around the base of the poster-board hat.

e. Along the top of the tin foil, cut out triangle wedges, spacing them about 1" (2.5 cm) apart.

f. Glue the tin foil around the base of the hat to make a crown around it.

g. Punch two holes towards the bottom on opposite sides of the hat.

h. Thread a 16" (40 cm) piece of string or yarn through each hole to tie under your chin. This will help your princess hat stay in place on your head.

i. Dress up in your favorite long dress and your newly created hat.

More Ideas

Create a wand for your costume by cutting a star shape out of cardboard and taping a pencil to it. Cover the whole thing with tin foil.

Make a poor rag dress to go over your beautiful dress by taking an oversized, plain, white T-shirt and tattering the bottom edge with scissors. Place small rips along the shoulders of the shirt. Using black fabric paint, paint on grease and soot smears. Tie a sash or belt around the waist. Pretend to be transformed into a beautiful princess by taking off the tattered dress to reveal your beautiful gown.

Cool Knight Costume

28

Cool Knight Costume

Materials

- Open-faced ski mask
- Large sheet of cardboard
- Strong scissors
- Large paper bag
- Tin foil
- Acrylic paints and paintbrush
- Glue
- Tape
- Stapler

Let's Do It

a. Cover the outside of the ski mask with tin foil, tucking the excess tin foil inside the mask and pressing it tightly.

b. Cut out a shield shape and a sword shape from the large sheet of cardboard, as well as a cardboard strip that is about 1.5" (4 cm) wide and 5" (12 cm) long.

c. Glue tin foil around the sword shape, tucking the excess foil around the back and taping it in place.

d. To make a handle for the shield, tape the strip of cardboard in the center of the back of the shield. Place tape along the top and along the bottom of the strip so that there is an opening in the middle to hold onto.

e. For the sword, cover the blade in tin foil and leave the cardboard handle.

f. Open the paper bag and cut the two sides off, leaving the front, back, and bottom intact. Cut a circle out of the bottom of the bag large enough to fit over your head.

g. Cover the paper bag completely with tin foil, gluing or stapling it in place.

h. Paint a symbol or picture on the front of the shield and allow it to dry completely.

i. Carefully place the body armor over your head to fit on your shoulders and place the covered ski-mask armor over your head. Arm yourself with your shield and sword for your newly designed knight costume.

More Ideas

Cover a hockey or football helmet with tin foil instead of using an open-faced ski mask for the head armor.

Create a family crest and place it on the front of the body armor. Divide the crest into four or five sections. In each section, draw a symbol that represents something important to your family.

Ceiling Giant and Beanstalk

Ceiling Giant and Beanstalk

Materials

- Thick rope
- Green construction paper
- Stapler
- Five sheets of white 11" x 14" (27 cm x 35 cm) paper
- Crayons
- Scissors
- Five paper fasteners
- Tacks, pins, or tape

Let's Do It

a. Measure a length of rope to reach from the ceiling to the floor.

b. Cut out large leaves from the green construction paper.

c. Staple the leaves to the rope to create a long, leafy beanstalk.

d. To make the giant, use one sheet of white paper to make his head, another sheet for the body, two sheets for the legs and boots, and the last sheet for both arms.

e. Draw the body parts on the paper and color them.

f. Cut the giant out. So the parts are moveable, attach the body parts together using paper fasteners.

g. Next, connect the giant to the top of the beanstalk by stapling the tip of his head to the top to the rope.

h. Position the giant's arms, so that they appear to be climbing down the beanstalk. Staple the hands in position.

i. Attach the beanstalk to the top of the wall or ceiling, using a method that you are comfortable with. Some suggestions might be tacks, pins, tape, etc.

More Ideas

Use another 11" x 14" paper to create the character of Jack. Draw, color, and cut him out from the paper and staple him towards the bottom of the beanstalk.

Make a smaller version of the Jack and the Beanstalk story by using a potato chip can. Cut green leaves out of construction paper and glue them around the can in layers, until completely covered. Place a small house at the top to represent the castle. Make the characters Jack and the giant out of construction paper. Glue them on the beanstalk to give the illusion of climbing down.

Pinocchio

Pinocchio

Materials

- Nine toilet-paper rolls
- Four paper fasteners
- Infant sized outfit
- One paper plate
- Markers or crayons
- One clothespin
- One pipe cleaner
- Tape

Let's Do It

a. Attach two toilet paper rolls together using a paper fastener. Press the fasteners through one at a time. Repeat this step twice so that there are two legs.

b. Tape three of the other toilet paper rolls together. This will be Pinocchio's body.

c. Connect the legs to the body with tape.

d. Use another paper fastener to connect a toilet paper roll to the top roll of the body. Repeat this step twice to create both arms.

e. Draw and color Pinocchio's face and hair on the paper plate, cutting a small hole in the center for the nose.

f. Tape the pipe cleaner to the back of the paper plate, at the top and the bottom.

g. Place the clothespin through the center hole in the plate and clip it onto the pipe cleaner at the back to hold it in place.

h. Tape the head to the top of the body you have created.

i. Dress Pinocchio in the infant outfit, socks, and mittens.

j. To make Pinocchio's nose grow, clip the clothespin to the tip of your finger and slide it in and out, while holding your new puppet.

More Ideas

To make the Pinocchio puppet into a marionette, attach string to the bottom of each arm and leg, joining the strings together at the top and placing them on a ruler or stick.

Put on a puppet show with your Pinocchio and while telling the story, make his nose grow every time he tells a lie.

Marshmallow Candy Houses

Marshmallow Candy Houses

Materials

- Jumbo marshmallows
- Confectioners sugar
- Water
- Craft sticks
- Graham crackers
- Candies for decoration
- Spoon or knife

Let's Do It

a. Build a cube using the marshmallows and craft sticks. Start with one marshmallow and insert a craft stick into the center. At the other end, place another marshmallow. Stick in other craft sticks, going in the opposite direction and up, placing a marshmallow on the other end of each craft stick, until you have your basic cube shape. (See diagram above.)

b. To make the roof of the house, place two craft sticks into a marshmallow at a point. Place the two sticks into two of the marshmallows at the top of the cube. Do the same thing on the other side. Place a craft stick in the center at the top to complete the house.

c. Combine four-parts icing sugar with one-part water. Mix well to make a very thick "glue-like" paste.

d. Spread the paste onto the craft sticks. Carefully, attach the graham cracker squares to make the walls and roof.

e. When the structure has had time to dry and is secure, use the rest of the paste to glue the candies on for decoration.

More Ideas

To add a chimney to the house, use eight toothpicks and four small marshmallows. Place a marshmallow on the ends of four of the toothpicks. Join them together using the remaining toothpicks. Place this structure into one of the top corner jumbo marshmallows. Cover with a thin fruit roll-up to create the chimney.

Melt marshmallows slightly and spread them along the roof, to create the look of snow.

Put a small amount of icing in a zipper plastic bag and use to decorate the candy house with windows and a door.

A Christmas Fairy Tale

Once upon a [alarm clock]

[Santa] and his [reindeer] could not [magnifying glass] the

little [castle] . The [princess] [crying face] because there

were no [present] under her [Christmas tree] .

A Christmas Fairy Tale

Materials

- Writing paper
- Pencil
- Poster board
- Packing tape
- Index or recipe cards
- Crayons or markers
- Magazine or personal pictures
- Construction paper
- Scissors

Let's Do It

a. Write a fairy tale or substitute Mrs. Claus and Santa's names into a familiar tale; also, change the setting and story to take on a more Christmas appearance.

b. Create a storyboard by cutting a large poster-board in half. Cut one half of the poster-board into equal-sized strips. Attach the strips to the other half of the poster board, using the packing tape, leaving a 2" (5 cm) space in between each strip. This will create pockets to place the story cards in. There will be extra strips left over.

c. Write your new story onto the index cards, one word per card, leaving a blank space at the bottom half of each card.

d. Cut out magazine pictures, or create pictures from construction paper, to replace words that can be read by a picture. Glue the pictures onto the index cards. For example, a picture of Santa can be used instead of writing out his name.

e. Place the story cards into the pockets of the storyboard to read and change while retelling the story.

More Ideas

Personalize your story by placing pictures of yourself, your family, your pets, etc., into the story at the appropriate times.

Hang the storyboard up and change the story or pictures often so there will always be something new to look at and read.

Snow Castles

Snow Castles

Materials

- Snow
- Water (if snow isn't sticky)
- Empty containers—ice-cream pails, milk cartons, plastic jugs, small plastic cups, etc.
- Liquid tempera paint or snow paint
- Large paint brush

Let's Do It

a. Using the empty containers, collect snow outside. Pack it very hard.

b. Tip the containers over onto level ground, keeping the snow packed together, with bigger snow blocks forming the base or bottom of the castle. Put two milk-carton snow towers on each side.

c. On top of the bigger snow formation, add snow from the small plastic cups to make the top of the castle.

d. Paint the snow castle.

More Ideas

Use large square containers to make a brick castle fort. Paint the bricks red and black.

Collect clean snow in a cup. Pour juice or jell-o water over it to make a homemade snow cone.

If no snow is available in your area, make sand castles in the same way.

Pumpkin Shell Play

Pumpkin Shell Play

Materials

- Orange frozen pizza container
- Poster board strip
- Paper
- Crayons or markers
- Scissors

Let's Do It

a. Cut triangle windows out of the middle of the frozen pizza container.

b. Draw Peter and his wife on paper.

c. Color the figures and cut them out.

d. Glue Peter on the outside of the container.

e. On the side of the container, cut a small slit and insert the strip of poster board through the slit.

f. Glue the wife inside the pumpkin-shell container on the edge of the poster board strip.

g. Move the poster board strip in and out to make the wife move.

Note: If you can't find an orange container, use a container of another color and paint it orange with orange acrylic paint. You may also use large paper plates.

More Ideas

Use the orange frozen pizza container to create a jack-o-lantern at Halloween. Cut a face out of the orange container and glue black tissue paper over the cut-out face parts.

Chant the nursery rhyme "Peter, Peter Pumpkin Eater," while you play with the container shell.

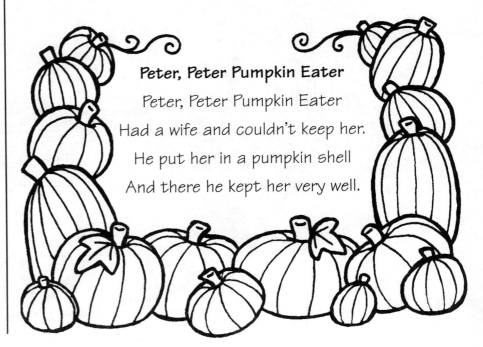

Peter, Peter Pumpkin Eater

Peter, Peter Pumpkin Eater

Had a wife and couldn't keep her.

He put her in a pumpkin shell

And there he kept her very well.

Insects and Spiders

Insects and Spiders

Fun Books to Read and Web Sites to Explore:

Carle, Eric. **The Grouchy Ladybug**. HarperCollins Publishers Inc., 1977.

Carle, Eric. **The Honeybee and the Robber**. Scholastic Inc., 1981.

Carle, Eric. **The Very Busy Spider**. Philomel, 1984.

Carle, Eric. **The Very Hungry Caterpillar**. Putnam Publishing Group, 1969.

Carle, Eric. **The Very Lonely Firefly**. Philomel, 1995.

Carle, Eric. **The Very Quiet Cricket**. Philomel, 1990.

Giganti Jr., Paul. **How Many Snails?** Mulberry Books, 1994.

Kirk, David. **Miss Spider's Tea Party**. Scholastic Inc., 1994.

Lobel, Arnold. **Grasshopper on the Road**. Harper, 1978.

McKissack, Pat. **Bugs!** Children's Press, 1988.

McNutty, Faith. **The Lady and the Spider**. HarperCollins Publishers, 1987.

Nielson, Claire and Doug Steer. **Snappy Little Bugs**. The Millbrook Press, 1992.

Pallotta, Jerry. **The Icky Bug Alphabet Book**. Charlesbridge, 1992.

Pallotta, Jerry. **The Icky Bug Counting Book**. Charlesbridge, 1992.

Soya, Kiyoshi. **The House of Leaves**. Philomel, 1987.

Stone, Rosetta. **Because A Little Bug Went Ka-choo!** Random House, 1975.

Web Sites:

Butterfly and Caterpillar Crafts
www.EnchantedLearning.com/crafts/butterfly/

Children's Butterfly Site
www.mesc.nbs.gov/butterfly/Butterfly.html

Insect Crafts
www.EnchantedLearning.com/crafts/insects/

The Official Eric Carle Web Site
www.eric-carle.com/

Spider Bags

Spider Bags

Materials

- Large, brown shopping bag
- White wax crayon
- Black tempera paint and paintbrush
- Tin foil
- Scissors
- Glue

Let's Do It

a. Draw a spider web on both sides of the bag. Use a white crayon and press firmly on the paper bag.

b. Paint over the whole bag with the black paint.

c. Cut out a spider shape from tin foil. You can trace or enlarge a pattern from page 72.

d. After the bag has dried, glue the tin foil spider onto the web.

More Ideas

Use your spider bag as a Halloween treat bag.

To make a spider web poster, use a large sheet of poster board. Draw a web with a white crayon and paint over it with the black paint. Glue on a tin foil spider and other construction-paper bugs caught in the web.

Make a smaller version using a lunch bag instead of a shopping bag.

Black Binder Spider

Black Binder Spider

Materials

- Black plastic flexible folder or binder cover
- Two wiggle eyes
- Hot glue gun
- Silver crayon or marker
- Scissors

Let's Do It

a. Draw a spider body, head, and eight legs on the folder cover.

b. Cut the parts out.

c. Glue the pieces together.

d. Glue the wiggle eyes onto the head of the spider.

e. Decorate with silver on the legs to create a hair-like effect.

f. Bend the legs in the middle to make it more realistic.

More Ideas

Using thick white string or yarn, create a large spider web for the spider. Use two large pieces of string and tie them together in the middle to create a "t." Start with a small piece of string and make a circle around the knot, tying it to the "t." Use a larger string and make a circle around the middle circle. Continue to build up until you have your web.

Make Halloween Spider Napkin Rings by cutting off a third of a toilet paper roll and painting it black. Cut a small spider from a flexible black folder cover. Glue it onto the toilet paper roll, decorating with small wiggle eyes.

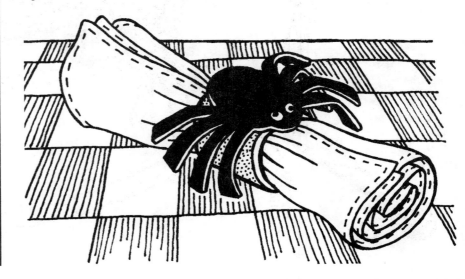

Milk Jug Bug

Materials

- Milk jug (gallon)
- Black acrylic paint
- Three pairs of old black tights or nylons
- Black construction paper
- Silver marker
- Glue
- One black pipe cleaner cut in half
- Stapler and staples

Let's Do It

a. Pour a small amount of paint into the milk jug. Put the lid on tightly and shake the paint well, until the inside is completely covered in the black paint.

b. Allow the paint to settle and dry for about 24 hours, then, shake it around vigorously one more time and allow it to dry.

c. Crumple up black construction paper and use it to fill up the legs of the black tights.

d. Staple two pairs of tights together at the top of the legs. Then attach them to the third pair also at the top of the legs.

e. Place the milk jug into the opening of the third pair of tights, pulling the tights up over the back of the jug and over the lid. Glue it in place over the lid.

f. Poke the pipe cleaners through the tights at the top to make the antennae.

g. Use silver marker to give your bug a face.

More Ideas

Create a black octopus by following the same steps, but use four pairs of tights and no antennae.

For a more polished look, stuff the nylons with paper and pull them through the milk jug handle, tipping the milk jug onto its side. Papier mâché over the whole thing and paint it black.

Butterfly Mask

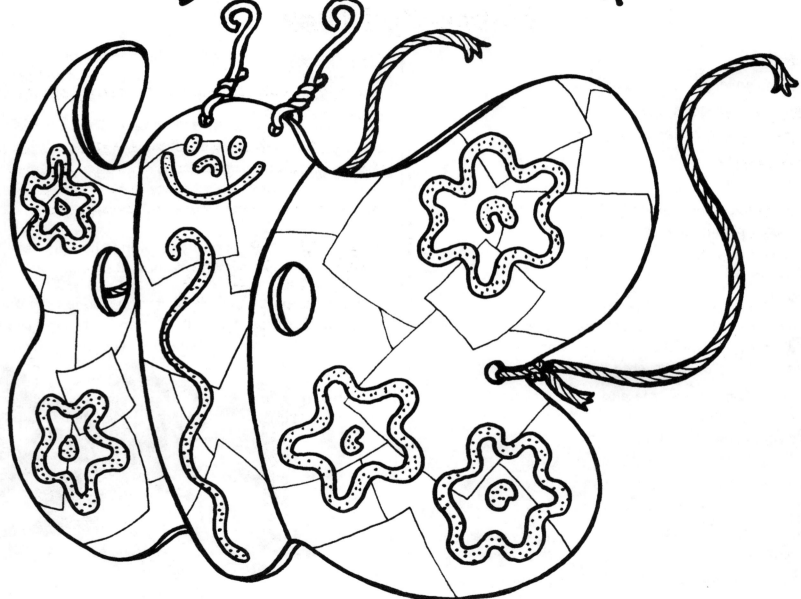

Butterfly Mask

Materials

- Scissors
- Empty (gallon) milk jug
- Various colors of tissue paper
- Glitter glue
- Glue
- One pipe cleaner cut in half
- Silver marker

Let's Do It

a. Cut the milk jug in half. Use the half of the milk jug without the handle on it. Cut it into the shape of a butterfly. (See diagram.)

b. On each wing of the butterfly, cut out eye holes.

c. Glue tissue paper of various colors to the wings and body of the butterfly.

d. Cut the eye holes out of the tissue paper.

e. Poke two holes at the top to fit the pipe cleaners through for the butterfly antennae.

f. Smear glitter glue over the tissue paper for decoration.

g. Use markers to decorate the face and the rest of the wings and body.

More Ideas

Glue a craft stick to the back to make the butterfly into a masquerade mask.

Create a ladybug mask by gluing red tissue paper over the whole mask and then cutting out black circles to glue on top. Draw the face with a black marker and use halves of a black pipe cleaner for the antennae.

Caterpillar Bag Metamorphosis

52

Caterpillar Bag Metamorphosis

Materials

- Large, yellow garbage bag
- Acrylic paint and paintbrush
- Scissors
- Five elastic bands
- Glue

Let's Do It

a. Cut the bottom of the garbage bag off and run scissors up each side, so that you have two sheets of large yellow plastic.

b. Smear different colors of paint over one sheet of the plastic.

c. Place the second sheet over the paint.

d. Roll the plastic up and secure it on each end and in the middle with the elastic bands.

e. Poke holes in each section so air is allowed in and the paint will dry. Allow paint to dry for about two or three weeks. (This time can be used to explain that it takes awhile for a caterpillar to change into a butterfly).

f. Leaving the middle elastic in place, remove all other elastic bands.

g. Open the plastic up, joining the ends on each side and glue them together.

More Ideas

Create a green caterpillar by rolling up a green garbage bag and securing it with elastic bands. Cut small pipe cleaner legs for the caterpillar and poke them into the bottom of the bag. Glue on a face made from construction paper.

Use pudding instead of paint when doing finger painting. Roll it up, then unroll it and let it dry in the open air.

Carpet Bug Box

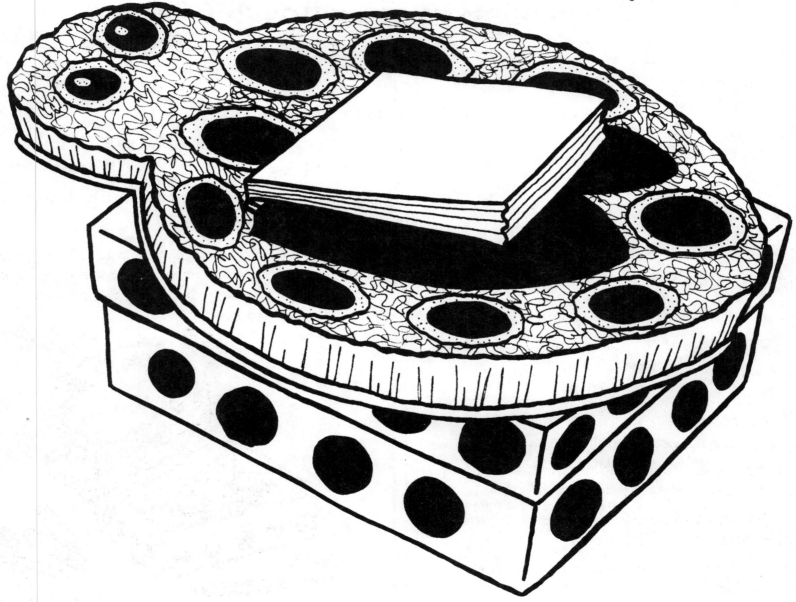

54

Carpet Bug Box

Materials

- Red carpet sample
- Craft knife
- Black felt
- Red glitter glue
- Empty boot box
- Red and black construction paper
- Glue
- Scissors
- Notepad

Let's Do It

a. Ask an adult to cut the carpet sample into the shape of a ladybug using the craft knife.

b. Cut circles out of the black felt, as well as two wing shapes joined together by a line in the middle.

c. Glue the wings down in the center of the bug, but leave the middle line open so a notepad can be stuck in between the carpet and the felt.

d. Glue the circles all over the ladybug as well as two smaller ones at the top for eyes.

e. Trace the spots with red glitter glue for a more dramatic look.

f. Glue red construction paper over the sides of the box. Cut out black construction paper circles and glue them on.

g. Glue the carpet to the top of the box.

More Ideas

Fill the ladybug box with craft supplies, markers and crayons, or bug-watching items.

Don't attach the box to the carpet. Instead, use the bug as a wall notepad hanger. Use a hot glue gun to attach a hook or large paper clip to the back of the carpet and hang it up.

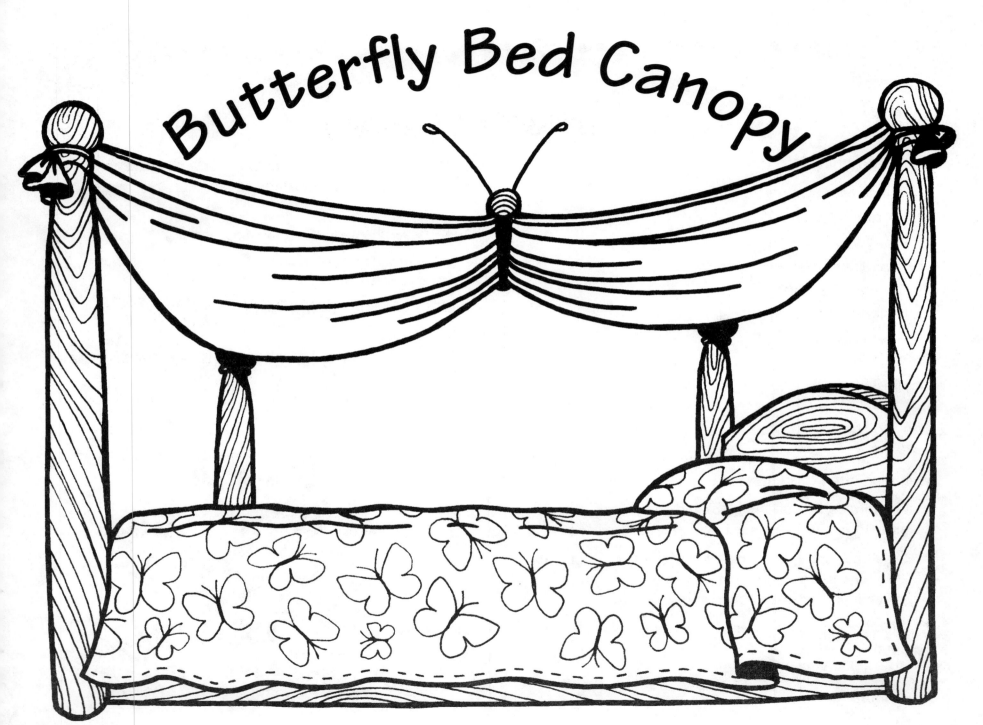

Butterfly Bed Canopy

Butterfly Bed Canopy

Materials

- Large cardboard packing tube
- Paint and paintbrush
- Knife
- Extra-large, flat, colored sheet
- Four elastic bands
- Two pipe cleaners

Let's Do It

a. Paint the cardboard tube and allow it to dry. If it isn't dark enough, give it a second coat of paint and let it dry.

b. In the middle of the tube, ask an adult to use a knife to make a vertical slit that doesn't quite go to each end of the tube.

c. Have an adult cut an identical slit on the opposite side of the tube.

d. Feed the large, flat, colored sheet through the slits in the tube, so that the tube is in the middle. The tube forms the body of the butterfly and the sheet forms the wings.

e. Push the pipe cleaner through the tube and twist it together to make the antennae. Do this with both pipe cleaners.

f. On the canopy posts of the bed, attach each wing corner with an elastic band.

More Ideas

To give the butterfly a tie-dye look, use a plain, white sheet. Soak the sheet in fabric dye and allow it to dry. Use another color of dye and only soak part of the sheet. Use as many colors as you would like.

If you don't have a canopy bed, but like butterflies, use a plain white flat sheet and fabric paint to paint butterflies all over the sheet. Allow time to dry, and sleep under your new sheet.

Lightweight material can be used instead of a large bed sheet.

Use 12" (30cm) square pieces of fabric and toilet paper rolls to make small versions of the butterfly canopy, and hang them around your room.

Bee Hive Flower Pot

Bee Hive Flower Pot

Materials

- Large drinking glass or vase
- Yellow and black clay
- Yellow and black pipe cleaners
- Small wiggle eyes
- Plastic wrap
- Scissors

Let's Do It

a. Roll strips of clay into snake-like coils. Make an even number of each color—yellow and black.

b. Wrap the coils around the vase or glass. Alternate between yellow and black. Press the ends together firmly and smooth all of it over.

c. Twist the yellow and black pipe cleaners together at the top to make small bees.

d. Cut out plastic wrap wings and twist them into the pipe cleaners.

e. Glue small wiggle eyes onto each bee.

f. Push the excess pipe cleaner at the bottom of the bees into the top clay coils.

g. Fill the vase with real or homemade flowers.

More Ideas

Use a Styrofoam egg carton, pipe cleaners, and gumdrops to create flowers for the center of your flowerpot. Cut out each egg cup and push a pipe cleaner stem into the center. Attach a gumdrop inside the pipe cleaner with glue to hold it in place.

Give the flowerpot more of a honeycomb look, by taking a plastic knife or spoon and smearing the colors together. Then carefully trace a honeycomb pattern into the clay.

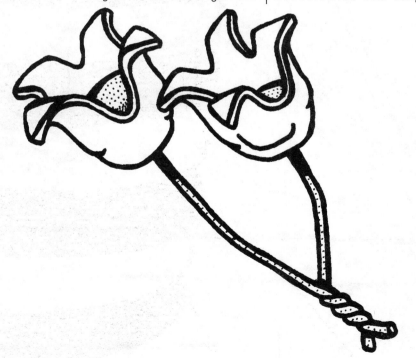

3-D Tissue Paper Bugs

3-D Tissue Paper Bugs

Materials

- Four milk jug caps
- Various colors of tissue paper, such as red, black, purple, pink, and yellow
- Rectangle box with a clear lid
- Glue
- Scissors
- Patterns of bug bodies from pages 72 and 73

Let's Do It

a. Cut out four spider bodies and 8 spider legs from black tissue paper. Glue eight legs around a milk jug lid. Glue one spider body onto the lid. Down the center of the body, place a small dab of glue. Lightly press another body onto it. Do the same with another body. Place the last body at the top.

b. Make a beetle in the same way as the spider, but make 6 legs instead of 8.

c. To make a ladybug, glue a black ladybug body onto the milk cap. Press on two red bodies. Dip small bits of black tissue paper into glue and drop onto the red tissue paper. Cut small black wings and glue them under the third body, so only a little bit shows on each side.

d. Cut out a butterfly from four or five different colors of tissue paper. Glue each butterfly onto the center of the milk cap, pressing the middle tightly and fluffing the wings with your fingers.

e. Place the milk cap bugs into the box and put the lid on, so they can be observed without too much direct handling.

More Ideas

Add in black tissue paper flies with plastic wrap wings and rolled tissue paper caterpillars to the collection.

If you can't find a box with a see-through lid, glue plastic wrap over the opening of a box or secure the plastic wrap with a large rubber band.

Pizza Box Bug Concentration

Pizza Box Bug Concentration

Materials

- Eight empty pizza boxes
- construction paper in a variety of colors—green, red, black, purple, pink, etc.
- Glue
- Scissors

Let's Do It

a. Decide on four different kinds of bugs you would like to make and make two matching bugs out of construction paper. The bugs can be as large as the inside of the pizza boxes.

b. On the outside of each lid, cut and glue green construction paper to cover it. Cut out matching paper flowers to glue in the center of each box. The outside of all eight boxes should be identical.

c. Place each bug inside a different box and close the lids, so you are unable to see them.

d. Mix the boxes up and lay them on the floor or table.

e. Take turns with a partner playing this bug memory game.

How To Play:

a. The first person lifts the lids of two of the boxes to try and find matching bugs.

b. If a match is found, the player gets to take the pair out, but close the lids of the boxes and leave them in place. The player then gets another turn.

c. If no match is found, the player closes the lids and the next player receives his/her turn.

d. Play until all four pairs have been found.

More Ideas

Learn how to spell the names of the bugs used in the game. Use four of the construction paper bugs and match them to their names written on paper and inserted into the boxes.

Instead of using construction paper, make bugs out of clay and play the game with matching clay insects.

Caterpillar Terrarium

Caterpillar Terrarium

Materials

- Aquarium
- Loose gravel
- Potting soil
- Small plants
- Large twig or branch
- Small twigs and branches
- Small dish of water
- Fresh grass
- Fuzzy caterpillar or powdered tempera paint and a cotton ball
- Screen top (available at pet stores)

Let's Do It

a. Cover the bottom of the aquarium with a thick layer of loose gravel.

b. Place a thin layer of potting soil over the top and plant several small plants in the soil.

c. Cover this with more loose gravel.

d. Put large and small twigs or branches over the top of the gravel.

e. Place a small dish of fresh water off to the side in the aquarium.

f. Add fresh grass every day, sprinkling it throughout, and placing a small pile in the corner.

g. Find a small fuzzy caterpillar or make a caterpillar from a stretched-out cotton ball decorated with powdered tempera paint and keep him comfy indoors in the terrarium.

h. Cover the terrarium with a screen and place it near a window or close to light.

More Ideas

If possible, add fresh water, flowers, grass, and twigs daily to help the caterpillar live in the terrarium long enough for it to spin a cocoon and change into a butterfly. Then, set it free.

To make a temporary bug collector, use a tall bowl or dish. Fill it with fresh grass and small twigs. Use an elastic band to hold netting or a screen in place at the top so that the bugs can't escape.

If you are interested in seeing the metamorphosis of the caterpillar to butterfly, you can buy a butterfly garden. Buterfly gardens are available in toy stores or educational supply stores.

Tree Top Honey Pot Game

Tree Top Honey Pot Game

Materials

- Four wire coat hangers
- Four small clothespins
- Four large brown pompons
- 12 small brown pompons
- Eight small wiggle eyes
- Small green garbage bags
- Packing tape
- Glitter glue in green and gold
- Glue
- Yellow paper
- Dice

Let's Do It

a. Place two coat hangers with the hooks facing opposite ends and tape the top end to form a figure A.

b. Do the same with the other two coat hangers. Place one set of hangers in the middle of the other hangers and tape them together at the top. (See diagram above.)

c. Place a small strip of glue along the four outside wires and cover the wire base with the green garbage bag. Make sure the bag is fitted tightly around the base and stuff the excess bag underneath.

d. Along the bag, where each of the four wires are underneath, print the numbers from 1–20 going up to the top of each.

e. Draw a small beehive on yellow paper and outline it in gold glitter glue. Cut out and attach the beehive to the top of the tree with glue.

f. To make the game pieces, glue a large brown pompon onto the small clothespin. Glue two small pompons on top for the ears, and one small pompon in the middle for a nose. Glue two small wiggle eyes above the nose.

g. Make four bear game pieces, one for each player.

How to Play

a. This game is for two to four players, with each player getting a clothespin bear game piece.

b. Place each of the game pieces at the base of one of the four wires and decide which person will go first.

c. The first person rolls the dice and moves his or her bear up to the matching number along the wire. He or she then clips it onto the wire. The next person takes a turn. Continue rolling the dice and moving up the appropriate number of spaces toward the hive.

d. The player to get to the top first can be declared the winner.

Butterfly Shirts

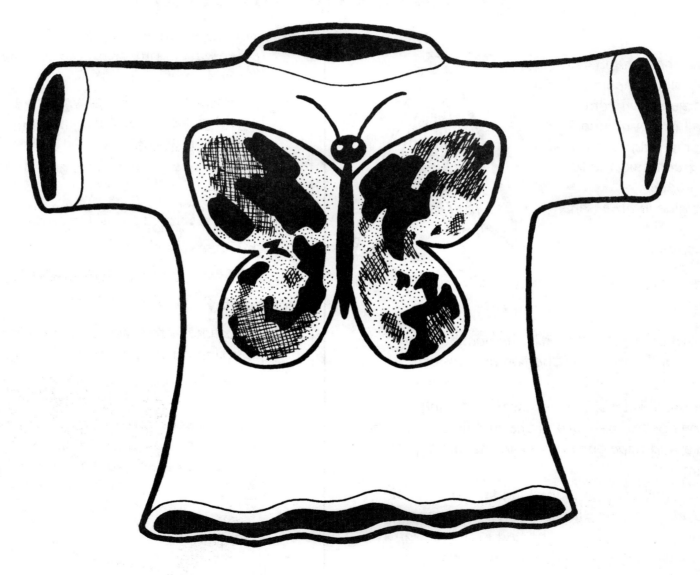

Butterfly Shirts

Materials

- Plain white T-shirt or sweatshirt
- Fabric paint in your favorite colors
- Paper
- Pencil
- Scissors
- Plastic wrap
- Small piece of cardboard

Let's Do It

a. Trace a pattern for a butterfly onto a piece of paper and cut it out.

b. Position the pattern in the center of the shirt and trace it on.

c. Place a piece of cardboard inside the shirt and then outline the pattern in fabric paint.

d. Cut a butterfly pattern out of plastic wrap, cutting it slightly smaller than the original pattern.

e. Place different colors of fabric paint onto the shirt in small dabs all over. Press the plastic wrap over the paint and smear it. Keep the dabs of paint inside the traced line about one inch. This will keep it from spilling outside the butterfly pattern.

f. Carefully remove the plastic wrap. If you're not happy with the way your shirt looks, repeat steps d-f.

g. Allow time for the paint to dry, then remove the cardboard and follow the directions on the fabric paint for washing.

More Ideas

Make tiny butterflies flying forward on the front, with the backs of the butterflies on the back of the shirt.

Leave the front and the back of the shirt plain, with butterflies going up the arms of the shirt.

Check your local craft store for sequins, glitter, and other exciting materials you can use with fabric paint.

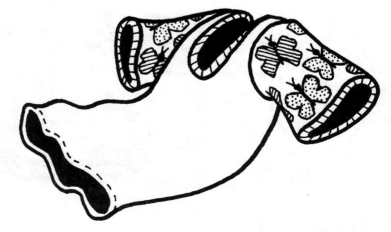

Spider and Web Cake

Spider and Web Cake

Materials

- Chocolate cake mix
- Chocolate frosting
- Black licorice strips and circles
- Whip cream
- Brown and green sprinkles
- 9" x 13" (22 cm x 33 cm) rectangle cake pan

Let's Do It

a. Follow the directions on the cake mix package to make a 9" x 13" cake.

b. When the cake has cooled, frost generously with chocolate icing.

c. In the top, left corner of the cake, spread whip cream along the edges to make two parts of a large triangle. Make two more diagonal lines going from the corner point towards the center of the cake. Join the lines together with wiggly lines to make the web design.

d. Cut one large round licorice and one small circle from licorice to make the spider head and body.

e. Cut 16 equal pieces of licorice to make the legs. Each leg will consist of one licorice going straight out and one piece at an angle.

f. Place the spider below the web on the cake.

g. Cover with brown sprinkles (dirt) and green sprinkles (grass).

More Ideas

Make a circle cake, ice it with chocolate frosting and then make the whole cake into a spider web by using whip cream to outline the cake and draw a "t" pattern, then connect with wiggly lines. Add a black licorice spider to the middle of the web cake.

Use more black licorice to create a fly trapped in the spider's web.

Use chocolate sandwich cookies to create small spiders. Insert the legs in the frosting in the middle. Add frosting eyes. Eat and enjoy this creepy crawly snack.

Small, Simple Bug Patterns

Use these patterns to make butterflies, beetles with six legs, spiders with eight legs, flies with wings, and ladybugs. Enlarge the patterns for the larger bug projects and keep the patterns as is for the projects where a variety of small bugs are used.

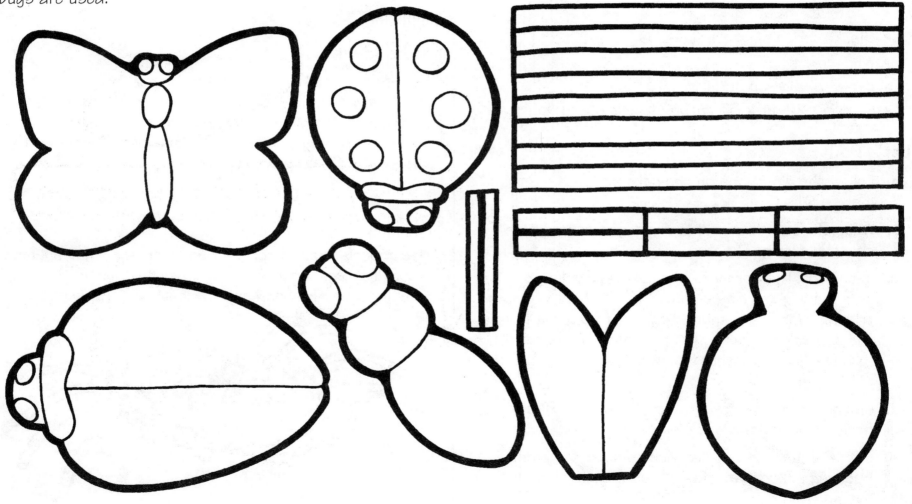

Small, Simple Bug Patterns (cont.)

Use these simple bug patterns to create bees, wasps, hornets, beetles, ants, and caterpillars. Enlarge the patterns as necessary.

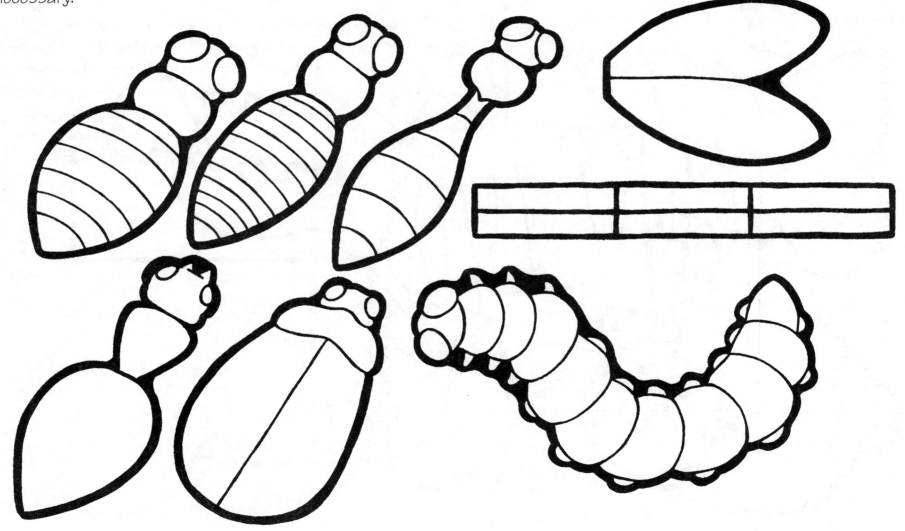

Dinosaurs

"I'm Hungry!"

Dinosaurs

Fun Books to Read and Web Sites to Explore

Aliki. **My Visit to the Dinosaurs**. Thomas Y. Crowell Company, 1969.

Arnold, Caroline. **Dinosaurs All Around**. Clarion Books, 1993.

Berenstain, Stan and Jan. **The Berenstain Bears and the Missing Dinosaur Bone**. Random House, 1980.

Grambling, Lois G. **Can I Have A Stegosaurus, Mom? Can I? Please!?** BridgeWater Books, 1995.

Johnson, Jay. **Dinosaurs!** (Know-It-Alls). McClanahan Book Company Inc., 1999.

Joyce, William. **Dinosaur Bob And His Adventure With the Family Lazardo**. A Laura Geringer Book, 1995.

Lauber, Patricia. **Living with Dinosaurs.** Aladdin Paperbacks, 1999.

Maynard, Christopher. **The Best Book of Dinosaurs**. Kingfisher, 1998.

Most, Bernard. **The Littlest Dinosaurs**. Harcourt Brace, 1993.

Most, Bernard. **Whatever Happened to the Dinosaurs?** Harcourt Brace Jovanovich, Publishers, 1984.

Nayer, Judy. **Living With Dinosaurs**. Aladdin Paperbacks, 1999.

Rohmann, Eric. **Time Flies**. Dragonfly, 1997.

Sanders, George. **The Mix and Match Book of Dinosaurs**. Simon and Schuster Children's Publishing Division, 1992.

Schwartz, Henry. **How I Captured a Dinosaur**. Orchard Books, 1993.

Skofield, James. **Detective Dinosaur**. HarperCollins Juvenile Books, 1998.

Web Sites:

Sites for Teachers—Dinosaurs
www.connectingstudents.com/themes/dinos.htm

Museum Victoria—Dinosaurs and Fossils
www.mov.vic.gov.au/dinosaurs/dinoactiv.stm

Dinosaur Picture Gallery
www.dinosauria.com/gallery/gallery.htm

Dinosaur Crafts
www.EnchantedLearning.com/crafts/dinosaurs/

T-Rex Hangman

Materials

- Two sheets of poster board
- Scissors
- Sticky tack (removable adhesive)
- Markers or crayons
- Pencil

Let's Do It

a. Cut out a hangman game board shape from white poster board.

b. Trace one of the dinosaur patterns from pages 78 and 79 onto the poster board. Use scissors to cut out the patterns.

c. Cut 60 equal-sized squares from the rest of the poster board.

d. On each square, write a letter of the alphabet. There are enough squares for you to write the whole alphabet twice and then have eight blank squares.

How to Play

a. Hang up your hangman board.

b. Think of a word that you want people to guess and use sticky tack to stick up enough blank squares for the letters in your word.

c. Players then take turns guessing letters. Whenever they guess a letter that is not in the word, part of the dinosaur body goes up under the hangman board. If a letter is guessed that is in the word, it is inserted in place of the blank square it takes.

d. The goal is to guess the word correctly before all of the dinosaur parts are hung up.

More Ideas

For small children, use the T-rex pieces as a puzzle.

For older children, already doing sentences, set the hangman up beside a chalkboard or whiteboard and draw blank spots to make a sentence or rhyme for them to guess.

Read books about dinosaurs, particularly about the Tyrannosaurus Rex, and play a hangman game using facts about the dinosaurs.

T-Rex Pattern Pieces

T-Rex Pattern Pieces (cont.)

Dinosaur Dig

Dinosaur Dig

Materials

- Large animal bones (can be obtained from a butcher, rancher, or meat packing plant)
- Bleach
- Water
- Thin wire thread
- Sandbox shovels or spoons

Adult Preparation

a. Soak bones in a mixture of 3 parts warm water and 1 part bleach to remove any skin fragments and odor. Then rinse with cold water and dry them off.

b. Bury the bones in your sandbox or in an area of loose dirt.

c. Invite your child to go on an archaeological dig.

Let's Do It

a. Dig up the bones with spoons or sandbox shovels.

b. Put all of the bones together on the floor in a shape that resembles a dinosaur skeleton.

c. Wrap thin wire thread around the bones to connect them and hold them in place.

More Ideas

For a smaller project, use chicken bones to create a mini-dinosaur replica by gluing the bones to construction paper in a skeletal shape.

Take pictures of your children's faces as they discover their first few bones in the sand.

Draw what you think the dinosaur skeleton would look like with its skin.

Before going on the dig, read books about dinosaurs to help familiarize the children with what a dinosaur skeleton would look like.

Poem Pictures

Apatosaurus liked to eat and eat, but don't give her a piece of meat. She wanted leaves and different trees. She took what she wanted and didn't say please. She stomped along and shook the ground. She was one of the biggest dinosaurs ever found. Apatosaurus!

blue

Poem Pictures

Materials

- Large roll of newsprint or wrapping paper or large poster board
- Markers and/or crayons
- Writing paper
- Pencil

Let's Do It

a. Write a poem or story about your favorite dinosaur.

b. Draw a large outline of the dinosaur your poem is about.

c. Use markers to print your poem or story around the outline of the dinosaur you have created.

d. Color him and give your poem picture a title.

More Ideas

Create a pictures and poems scrapbook. Use an ordinary scrapbook and take poems that you have written, or poems that you like, and draw a picture outline to go with them. Then, copy the poem around the picture.

Create a poem about a fierce, meat-eating T-rex, and if you are unable to draw an outline of one, find a picture on the internet or in a coloring book that you can cut out and print around.

Write a poem that follows a word pattern. For example:

_____
one noun

_____   _____
adjective   adjective

_____   _____   _____
verb   verb   verb

_____
four-word descriptive phrase

_____
one noun

"I'm Hungry!" T-Rex Game

"I'm Hungry!"

"I'm Hungry!" T-Rex Game

Materials

- Four sheets of tag board paper or two sheets of poster board
- Crayons or markers
- Scissors
- Glue or tape
- Dinosaur patterns on pages 112 and 113
- Dice

Let's Do It

a. Using two sheets of tag board or two equal rectangle sizes of poster board, draw the face of a T-rex on one sheet.

b. Cut out an opening for the mouth.

c. Glue or tape the edges of the two sheets together, leaving the inside open so smaller dinosaurs will fit inside the opening.

d. Using crayons or markers, color the face of the T-rex.

e. Use the remaining paper to make small dinosaurs that will fit in the mouth of the T-rex.

How to Play

a. Each player starts off by rolling a die and saying, "I'm hungry for _____ dinosaurs." (The number rolled on the dice is the number said in the blank).

b. Count out that number of small dinosaurs and place them in the mouth of the T-rex.

c. Continue until all of the dinosaurs are used up.

More Ideas

To play the game with numbers above six, make number cards instead of rolling the die. Pick a card and place that number of small dinosaurs into the mouth of the T-rex.

To change the game to an alphabet recognition game, make 26 small dinosaurs and cut 26 small square cards. Label each dinosaur with a letter of the alphabet and label each card with a letter. Pick a card and then find the matching letter on a dinosaur to place in the mouth of the T-rex.

Paper Collage

Paper Collage

Materials

- One piece of large white paper
- Grey construction paper
- Glue
- Scissors
- Markers
- Pencils

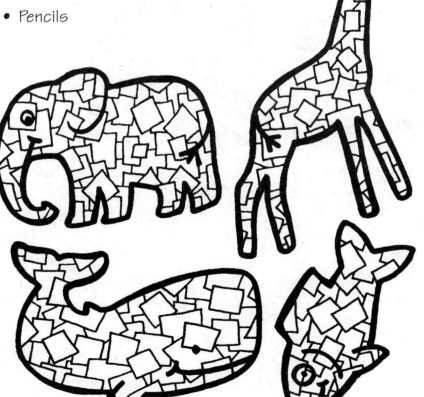

Let's Do It

a. Outline a dinosaur figure on the white paper.

b. Cut small squares from the construction paper.

c. Glue the squares overlapping each other onto the dinosaur outline. Cover the whole dinosaur.

d. Use a marker to outline the eyes and the mouth.

e. Cut out the dinosaur.

More Ideas

Create a dinosaur scene with paper collage trees, ponds, and rocks.

Make animal collages by outlining your favorite animal and cutting small squares of construction paper to glue on.

Plyboardasaurus Theme Park

Plyboardasaurus Theme Park

Materials

- Large sheet of plywood
- Green acrylic paint
- Plastercine in a variety of colors
- Blue hair gel
- Rocks
- Craft sticks
- Tacky glue
- Small dinosaur figures

Let's Do It

a. Paint the plywood green and allow it to dry completely.

b. Using blue hair gel, create a small pond in the middle.

c. Place rocks around the edges of the pond and all over the plywood.

d. Plastercine and craft sticks can be used to build a roller coaster. Place small drops of plastercine on the plywood and push the craft sticks into it.

e. Glue craft sticks together to create a long bridge and join this to the craft sticks standing up.

f. Small dinosaur figures can be used to decorate or to play with on your plywood park.

More Ideas

Make playground equipment to add to the park, such as, a slide made out of craft sticks and tinfoil, or a swing set made from craft sticks and strong string.

Once the roller coaster is stable, use small cars to drive on the track. If tacky glue isn't holding well enough, use a hot glue gun.

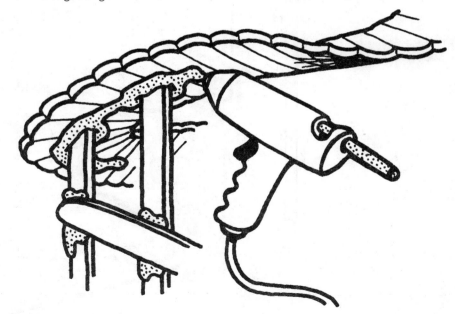

Dinosaur Cookie Cake

Dinosaur Cookie Cake

Materials

- Large saucepan
- Cookie sheet
- Spatula
- Wax paper
- 6 cups (685 g) of quick rolled oats (not instant)
- 1 cup (237 mL) of butter
- 3½ cups (400 g) of sugar
- 6 tbsp. (80 mL) Cocoa
- 1 cup (237 mL) of milk
- 1½ tsp. (7 mL) vanilla
- Raisins
- Butter knife and a spoon

Let's Do It

a. With the help of an adult, combine butter, sugar, cocoa, milk, and vanilla in a large saucepan. Stir until melted.

b. Remove from heat and add the oatmeal. Mix until it is completely moistened.

c. Using a spatula, place all of the chocolate-covered oatmeal onto a cookie sheet covered with wax paper. Allow it to cool so it can be handled safely.

d. Form the oatmeal into a dinosaur shape using a knife and spoon. Make a large body and oval shaped head. Allow time for it to harden.

e. Decorate your dinosaur cookie using raisins for eyes, teeth, and claws.

More Ideas

Use green frosting to spread over the whole cookie. Add raisins for eyes and white icing to make teeth and claws.

To make smaller dinosaur outlines, press the cookie batter onto a cookie sheet. Using a dinosaur cookie cutter, press the cutter all over the cookie sheet and allow time to cool and harden. Cut squares around each outline and serve.

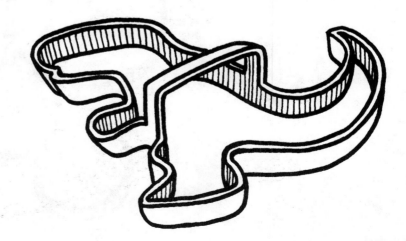

Plastic Pail Apatosaurus

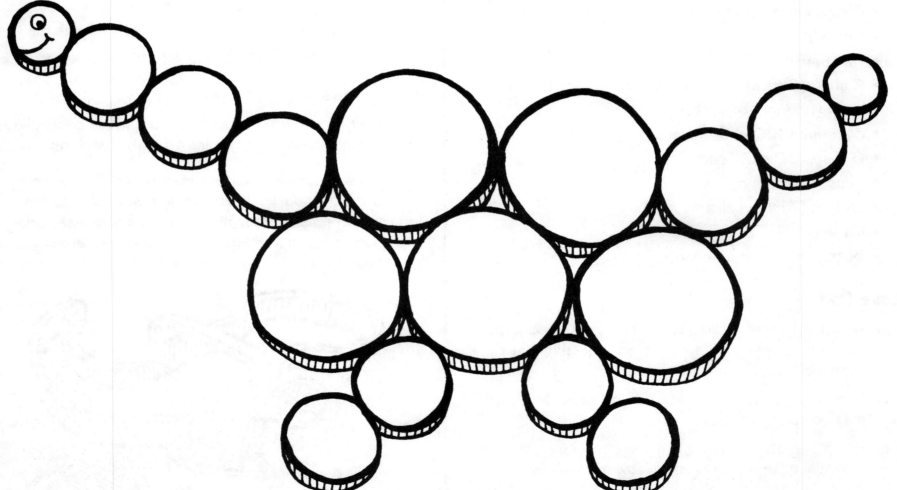

92

Plastic Pail Apatosaurus

Materials

- Plastic lids from five ice-cream pails, thirteen margarine containers and two smaller containers
- Green felt
- Glue
- Hot glue gun
- Scissors
- Stapler and staples

Let's Do It

a. To make the neck of the Apatosaurus, use three margarine container lids placed side by side by side and staple the edges together. One smaller lid can be used as the head and stapled at the top of the neck.

b. The body can be made by five ice-cream pail lids with three at the bottom and two on top. Staple them together and place the neck in the opening at the top, where the third lid should be placed.

c. Make the tail using two margarine lids and a small lid at the end.

d. Each leg is made of two margarine lids and stapled to the bottom of the body.

e. Before moving the Apatosaurus, fill in the cracks around the lids with hot glue. Allow it to dry.

f. Flip it over, and use hot glue to do the same on the opposite side.

g. Cut green felt to cover the lids. You may want to use extra lids to trace a circle pattern and then cut the amount of circles that you will need to cover the lids.

h. Glue the green felt over the lids.

More Ideas

Instead of green felt, give the dinosaur a shinier look by using green, plastic garbage bags to cover the body. Use green construction paper for a more matte finish.

To create a wall hanging of the Apatosaurus, use hot glue to stick two paper clips towards the top at the back and hang it on a wall.

Papier Mâché Dinosaurs

94

Papier Mâché Dinosaurs

Materials Needed for All Dinosaurs

- Garbage bags
- Water
- Tape
- Scissors
- Newspaper and plain paper
- Boxes
- Flour
- Mixing bowls
- Stapler
- Paint and paintbrush

Let's Do It

a. Choose a dinosaur and construct the shape using boxes and crumpled-up newspaper.

b. Cover the whole dinosaur with garbage bags before you papier mâché. This will prevent the boxes from getting soggy.

c. To make the thick paste, mix two parts flour with one part water. If the paste is too runny, mix in more flour.

d. Dip strips of newspaper into the paste and cover the entire surface of the dinosaur. Allow at least 24 hours for it to dry.

e. Give the dinosaur a second coat of papier mâché, using plain paper instead of newspaper and allow it to dry completely.

f. Paint and decorate your dinosaur.

Tyrannosaurus Rex Materials

- Large stereo box
- Newspaper
- One Styrofoam cup
- One four-liter, rectangular, vinegar jug
- Packing tape
- Four cereal boxes
- Two toilet paper rolls
- Large sheet of cardboard

Let's Do It

a. Open up both ends of the cereal boxes and tape two together. Stuff the inside with newspaper. Do the same with the other two.

b. Cut two large feet from cardboard and attach them to the bottom of each cereal box leg with packing tape.

c. The body can be formed from a large stereo box that is taped well to the legs of the dinosaur.

d. The toilet paper rolls can each be taped to the front of the box, to make small arms. Claws made of cardboard can be attached to the toilet paper rolls.

e. Cut the top off of a four-liter rectangular jug and cut a mouth in the middle.

f. Attach the jug to the bottom of the styrofoam cup using tape and then tape it to the top of the stereo box for the head and neck.

g. Proceed to instruction b in the first column.

Papier Mâché Dinosaurs *(cont.)*

Apatosaurus Materials

- Paper towel roll
- Two garbage bags (any color)
- Large plastic juice jug
- Newspaper
- Tape
- Large blue garbage bag
- Large shallow box
- Green tissue paper
- Two black pompons

Let's Do It

a. Stuff a garbage bag with newspaper for the body of the Apatosaurus and another garbage bag, thinly stuffed, will be used for the tail.

b. Tape the tail to the back of the body.

c. Using tape, attach a paper towel roll to the front of the body at the top of the neck.

d. The head of the Apatosaurus is made from a plastic juice jug with the cap of the jug as its mouth. Tape this well to the neck of the apatosaurus.

e. Starting with c, follow the instructions on page 95, for making papier mâché.

f. After the paint is dry, glue folded tissue paper to the end of the mouth and black pompons where the eyes would be.

g. Spread the blue garbage bag inside and outside of the shallow box.

h. Place the Apatosaurus in the box, to give the effect of standing in water.

Papier Mâché Dinosaurs (cont.)

Triceratops Materials

- Eight milk cartons
- Three medium-sized boxes
- One large cereal box
- Two paper-towel rolls
- Newspaper
- Packing tape or masking tape
- Cardboard
- Egg-carton cups

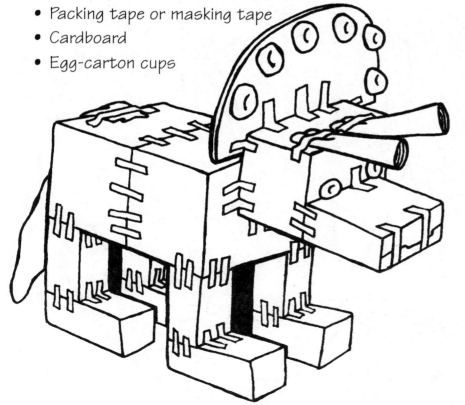

Let's Do It

a. Push the tops of all eight milk jugs in, or cut them off completely.

b. Tape two milk cartons together, with one lying flat and one standing on top to make a leg. Make four legs.

c. Tape two of the medium-sized boxes together to make the body, and attach them with tape to the legs of the Triceratops.

d. Tape the third box to the body for the head.

e. On top of the head, place cardboard cut in the shape of a large fan. Place egg-carton cups at the top for the scales.

f. Stuff the cereal box with newspaper and attach it for the mouth.

g. Use paper-towel rolls for the horns and two more egg-carton cups to make the eyes. These are taped on to the front of the head.

h. Starting with c on page 95, follow the instructions for making papier mâché.

Cracked Dinosaur Eggs

Cracked Dinosaur Eggs

Materials

- Two Styrofoam egg-carton cups
- White fun-tac or silly putty
- Two washed egg shells
- Tacky glue
- Small dinosaur figure
- Silver glitter glue

Let's Do It

a. Using the palm of your hand, push down on the eggshells to break them into smaller pieces.

b. Smear tacky glue over the outside of the egg-carton cups and place the broken eggshell pieces over top of the cups to cover them. Allow it to dry completely.

c. Spread glitter glue over the glued eggshells for decoration.

d. Place the openings of the two eggshell cups together and put a small dinosaur figure in the middle.

e. Join the cups with white silly putty.

f. Break open the egg by removing the silly putty to find the dinosaur inside.

More Ideas

Make a nest for your dinosaur egg using small sticks and large leaves.

Make a balloon-sized egg by gluing strips of paper to a blown-up oval balloon covered in Vaseline. Then glue crushed eggshells over the paper. Poke a pin into the balloon at the top to break it. Decorate the eggshells by painting them or covering them with glitter.

Deck of Dinosaurs

apatosaurus

Deck of Dinosaurs
(Concentration)

Materials

- An old deck of playing cards or small index cards
- Thick paper cut in 52 pieces the same size as the playing cards
- Glue
- Scissors
- Crayons or markers
- Old magazines or books about dinosaurs or patterns from pages 112 and 113

Let's Do It

a. Glue thick paper over the numbers and faces on the playing cards so that nothing can be seen.

b. Cut out and glue, or draw, 26 different pictures of dinosaurs on 26 of the covered cards.

c. On the remaining 26 cards, print the names of the dinosaurs pictured on the cards.

How to Play

a. Place the cards side-by-side with words and pictures facing down flat.

b. The first player turns over two cards.

c. If the player matches a dinosaur picture with the correct name, they take that pair and can take another turn.

d. If no match is found, the cards are turned back over and the next player takes a turn.

e. When all the pairs of cards are taken, the person with the most pairs may be declared the winner.

More Ideas

For children unable to read or recognize dinosaur names, glue or draw 26 matching pictures in place of the names.

To use only the more familiar dinosaurs, half of the deck would then be more appropriate. Find 13 of the more commonly known dinosaurs and draw or cut out pictures and glue them on the cards. Then, print the names of those 13 dinosaurs.

Use the cards to play a variation of Go Fish by fishing for pictures and words that match.

Long Neck Growth Chart

Long Neck Growth Chart

Materials

- Measuring tape
- Markers
- Large sheet of poster board
- Scissors
- Clear tape

Let's Do It

a. Cut the poster board in half lengthwise.

b. Take one half of the poster board and cut a third of it off of one end. You will not need the smaller piece.

c. Tape the long piece of poster board to the next size of poster board, so that it forms an "L" shape.

d. Draw and color a long neck on the poster board with the neck and head extending over most of the long poster board and the body and legs crammed into the base of the "L" formation.

e. When hanging the growth chart, the bottom should be two feet off of the floor.

f. Label the growth chart, starting at two feet, from the bottom up. Mark the growth chart at every inch.

More Ideas

If a different animal is preferred for the chart, follow the above steps but replace the Brontosaurus picture with that of a giraffe, ostrich, or other long-necked animal.

Use the paper collage idea suggested on pages 86 and 87 and glue it to the poster board. Then, measure and mark it for your growth chart.

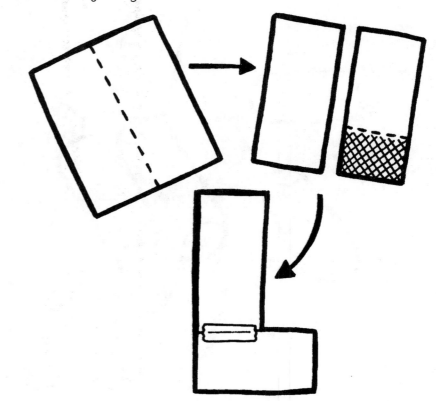

Foam Fossils

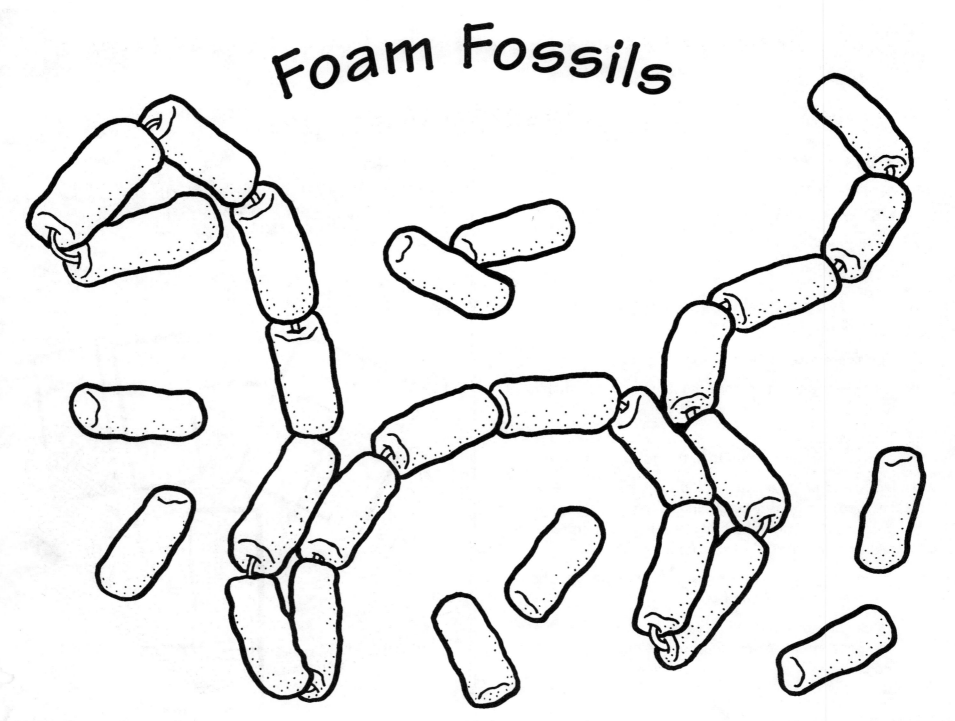

Foam Fossils

Materials

- Thin craft wire
- White packing foam
- Craft scissors

Let's Do It

a. Cut a two-foot long strip of thin craft wire for each foam fossil to be made.

b. Thread the wire through the middle of the foam, using enough foam pieces to cover the wire completely.

c. Bend and twist the middle or end of the wire to give the fossil the shape you desire.

d. Push the ends of the wire into foam pieces so that no wire is showing or sticking out.

More Ideas

Create a full-scale foam fossil dinosaur by attaching approximately 25 of the foam fossils together with more of the thin craft wire, using packing foam pieces in between the fossils.

Toothpicks can be used instead of the thin wire for a more rigid and less flexible look to each fossil.

Visit your local library and check out books about fossils. Read the books together to learn about fossils and see what a real one looks like.

Long Neck Dinosaur Delight

Long Neck Dinosaur Delight

Materials

- Large bowl
- Ice-cream scoop
- Ice cream
- One large banana, peeled
- Whip cream
- Blue food coloring
- Blue freezer pops
- Two raisins
- Chocolate chips
- Sprinkles
- Spoon

Let's Do It

a. In a large bowl, scoop in ice cream and place a peeled banana sticking out in the center.

b. Mix in a small drop of blue food coloring into the whip cream and spread that on top of the ice cream.

c. Use the two raisins to give the banana long neck dinosaur eyes. Lightly push the raisins into the top of the banana.

d. Open the blue freezer pops and squeeze them onto the whip cream all around the dinosaur.

e. Top with sprinkles and chocolate chips.

f. Grab a spoon and enjoy!

More Ideas

If you love the taste of chocolate, top the ice cream with chocolate sauce before you spread on the blue whip cream. Then, decorate with your favorite blue candy covered chocolate treats instead of sprinkles.

Make your own blue freezer pops with blue raspberry juice frozen in ice cube trays.

Garbage Bag Puppet

Garbage Bag Puppet

Materials

- Two green garbage bags
- Newspaper
- Tape
- Stick or ruler
- Brown felt
- Glue
- Scissors

Let's Do It

a. Stuff one garbage bag with crumpled up newspaper and shape it into a long dinosaur head.

b. Close the bottom of the bag aroung the stick and tape it off.

c. Decorate the dinosaur head with eyes cut out of the brown felt and triangle scales cut from the second garbage bag.

More Ideas

Create a T-rex and a long neck from garbage bags. Act out a dinosaur chase.

For smaller puppets, use a large, green sock to make a hand puppet.

Make a puppet stage by covering a table with a sheet. Sit behind the table, store your puppets underneath, and put on a puppet show. Invite friends and family to come and watch the production.

Fossil Cookies

Fossil Cookies

Materials

- Medium mixing bowl
- ½ lb. (227 g) of butter or margarine
- ½ cup (60 g) of confectioners sugar
- 6 tbsp (30 g) of brown sugar
- 1 egg yolk
- 2½ cups (285 g) of flour
- Craft sticks
- Cookie sheet
- Oven

Let's Do It

a. Knead together the butter, icing sugar, brown sugar, and egg yolk, mixing in flour until crumbly.

b. Roll the dough out and cut into 2" (5 cm) squares.

c. Place three craft sticks together, joining them at one end. Press the sticks into each cookie to create a print.

d. Bake at 350° until the edges are golden.

More Ideas

Make different imprints in the cookies. Collect and clean different turkey or chicken bones, using bleach. Press the dried bones into the cookies.

Make large dinosaur fossil imprints in clay by pressing large animal bones from cattle, deer or moose, into formed clay. Allow time to harden.

Dinosaur Patterns

Dinosaur Patterns (cont.)

Animals

Animals

Fun Books to Read and Web Sites to Explore:

Barrett, Judi. **Animals Should Definitely Not Wear Clothing**. Aladdin Books, 1989.

Base, Graeme. **Animalia**. Harry N. Abrams Inc., 1986.

Campbell, Rod. **Dear Zoo**. Four Winds Press, 1982.

Crebbin, June. **Cows in the Kitchen**. Scholastic Inc., 1999.

Howe, James. **Horace and Morris but Mostly Dolores**. Scholastic Inc., 2000.

Krause, Robert. **Leo the Late Bloomer.** Windmill Books, 1971.

Lee, Kate. **Snappy Little Colors**. The Millbrook Press, Inc., 1999.

Lee, Kate. **Snappy Little Numbers**. The Millbrook Press, Inc., 1999.

Munsch, Robert. **Alligator Baby**. Scholastic Canada Ltd,. 1997.

Palatini, Margie. **Moosetache**. Scholastic Inc., 1997.

Rosen, Michael. **Poems for the Very Young**. Kingfisher, 1993.

Rosen, Michael. **We're Going on a Bear Hunt**. Margaret K. McElderry Books, 1989.

Steer, Dugald. **Snappy Little Farmyard**. The Millbrook Press, Inc., 1999.

Wood, Don and Audrey. **The Little Mouse, the Red Ripe Strawberry, and the Big Hungry Bear**. Child's Play (International) Ltd., 1995.

Web Sites:

Sea World Animal Information Database
www.seaworld.org

National Wildlife Federation
www.nwf.org

Kokomo—Howard County Public Library
www.kokomo.lib.in.us/csd_animals.html

Environmental Education—Endangered Species
http://eelink.net/EndSpp/

Lazy Lounger

116

Lazy Lounger

Materials

- Large, fluffy pillow
- Small, clean car tire
- Large, white bed sheet
- Black fabric paint or permanent marker
- Ribbon
- Hot glue gun

Let's Do It

a. Place the pillow inside the middle of the tire.

b. Make spots all over the bed sheet with fabric paint or marker and let dry.

c. Cover the tire and pillow with the bed sheet.

d. Use a hot glue gun to attach the bed sheet to the bottom of the tire along the edge, making sure to have enough sheet on top, so it will give a little when a dog is sitting on it.

e. Decorate the top of the lounger by gluing on little bows made of ribbon.

f. Store your stuffed animals on this cozy chair or use it for yourself.

More Ideas

For an outside tire lounger, cover the material in clear plastic or use a sturdy, large, white garbage bag and glue black garbage-bag spots on top.

To make a tire swing, paint the tire with white outdoor paint, leaving black spots from the tire showing through. Attach a sturdy swing rope. Visit your local hardware store for the materials needed to hang the swing from a tree or swing set.

Paw Print Border

118

Paw Print Border

Materials

- Two colors of acrylic paint
- Wall
- Your hands or feet
- Vaseline

Let's Do It

a. With permission from your parents, make a fist and lightly cover the part of your fist where your little finger is with Vaseline.

b. Dip your fist into one of the paint colors and press it against the wall. Continue to make this pattern in a line.

c. Wash the paint off of your fist and then lightly rub Vaseline on your index fingertip.

d. Dip the tip of your index finger in the same color of paint and go back and put small toe prints above the fist footprints.

e. Make bear paws by dipping your palm and tips of your fingers (not including your thumb) in the second color of paint and press prints all over the wall.

f. Wash hands well and allow time for the paint on the wall to dry.

More Ideas

Make small bird tracks, by dipping your thumb into paint and pressing thumbprints on the wall. For the bird toe claws, dip the edge of your nail into paint and attach three small lines to the thumbprint in the shape of a "w."

Instead of decorating an entire wall, decorate a pegboard with feet and paw prints.

Make paw print wrapping paper by decorating paper in the same way.

Use fabric paint and decorate a plain, white bed skirt, sheets, and comforter to create a new look in your bedroom.

Animal Organizers

Animal Organizers

Materials

- Four empty large cereal boxes
- Large sheets of black construction paper
- White paper
- Crayons or markers
- Scissors
- Glue

Let's Do It

a. Cut the tops off of the cereal boxes and cut an opening to halfway down one of the skinny sides of each box.

b. Cover the three non-cut sides of the boxes by gluing the black construction paper over it.

c. Using the white construction paper and crayons, draw and color animal faces large enough to cover the half-side of the cereal boxes.

d. Cut the animal faces out and glue them on.

e. Decorate the black construction paper with white spots or stripes, depending on the animal.

f. Store your papers, magazines or homework inside the organizer boxes.

More Ideas

Instead of paper faces, make sock puppet faces to attach to the cereal boxes.

Attach a paper tail to the back of each of the animals.

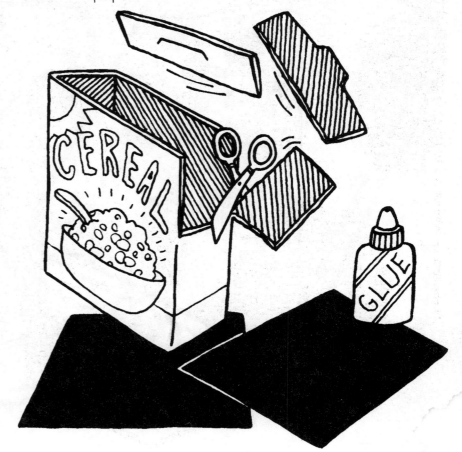

Animal Alphabet Tiles

K

k

L

l

M

m

Animal Alphabet Tiles

Materials

- Self adhesive wall tiles
- Wall
- Acrylic paint and paintbrush
- Animal alphabet stickers
- Measuring tape

Let's Do It

a. Read the directions on the back of the wall tiles carefully before beginning this project.

b. Measure the wall you are applying the tile border to and figure out how many tiles you will need. For example, if the wall requires 30 tiles, 2 extra tiles can be placed on each end, with the 26 alphabet tiles in the middle.

c. Review or teach the alphabet by painting each letter on one of the 26 tiles.

d. Find an animal sticker to fit with each letter of the alphabet and carefully press it onto the correct tile.

More Ideas

Instead of tiles, use a plain wallpaper border. Paint the border with a base color to go with the room. Then, draw and paint on alphabet letters and animals to go with each letter.

If you do not want to apply anything permanent to the wall, use the removable animal stickers and alphabet letter stickers.

Cover a small table or desk with the tiles instead of using a wall.

Paper Bag Rider

Paper Bag Rider

Materials

- Crumpled-up newspaper
- One large brown paper bag
- Empty wrapping paper roll
- Two small brown paper bags
- Glue
- Tape
- Coarse yarn
- White and black felt

Let's Do It

a. Stuff the large paper bag with crumpled-up newspaper.

b. Push the wrapping paper roll into the bag opening and tape the end shut with the roll sticking out.

c. Form two ears out of the small paper bags. Attach them to the large bag.

d. Cut eyes and nose holes from the felt and glue onto the head of the horse.

e. Strips of coarse yarn can be used to make the horse's mane. Glue the yarn in the middle of the ears and down the back.

More Ideas

Make a zebra by painting the bags with black and white stripes. Use black yarn to make the mane of the zebra.

For a stronger riding pole, use a larger willow stick instead of a wrapping paper roll.

Kangaroo Pocket Pouch Pet Treats

Pet Treats

126

Kangaroo Pocket Pouch Pet Treats

Materials

- Cardboard sheet
- Back pocket cut from old pants
- Paint or markers
- Strong scissors
- Pet treats
- Fabric glue

Let's Do It

a. Cut out a kangaroo figure from the cardboard sheet.

b. Decorate the kangaroo with paint or markers.

c. Use the paint or markers to color the pocket and label it with the words "Pet Treats."

d. Apply glue to the edges of the pocket and press it in the middle of the kangaroo. Allow the glue to dry.

e. Insert your pet's favorite treats into the pocket.

More Ideas

Organize craft items in different pocket pouches. Use an old button-up shirt and hang it up on a hanger, buttoned closed. On the back of the shirt, glue on four pockets to make pouches. Label each pouch with pencils, glue, or markers, etc. Hang it in the closet until you need it.

Button an old jean jacket on a hanger. Sew the bottom of the jacket shut. Decorate the back of the jacket with markers or fabric paint. Use the jacket hanger as a laundry bag or a place to put unused clothes.

Skunk in a Jar

128

Skunk in a Jar

Materials

- Large empty pickling jar and lid
- Black and white glass paint
- Make-up sponge
- White paper tag
- Thick yarn
- Artichoke hearts
- Sardines
- Pickling spice

Let's Do It

a. Sponge paint the outside of the jar with white on top and black on the bottom.

b. Allow the paint to dry completely.

c. In the jar, mix smelly items like artichoke hearts with sardines and pickling spice.

d. Seal the jar with the lid.

e. Tie a piece of thick yarn around the lid of the jar and attach a white tag with the words "Skunk in a Jar."

f. Discard the jar after 15 days or the skunky smell may take a long time to remove from a room.

More Ideas

Give the skunk in a jar to a friend with a note that says "Do you dare unleash the skunk in a jar, the smell might make your eyes water and tear. I hope this jar makes you smile a little. I'm giving it to you to bring you some cheer."

Make pickles by placing washed cucumbers in the jar with dill, garlic, pickling salt, sugar and vinegar. Fill to the top with cold water and seal the jar. Wait several weeks before opening and eating.

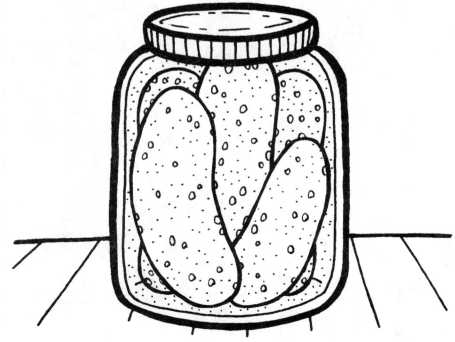

Dog House Activity Center

SPIKE

pencils

a b c

CHALK

Dog House Activity Center

Materials

- Small dog house
- Hot glue gun or tacky glue
- Block stacking boards
- Large drawing paper
- Chalkboard
- Plastic pencil case that closes tightly
- Puzzles that fit tightly into their boards
- White boards

Let's Do It

a. Glue block stacking boards over half of the roof of the doghouse.

b. On the other half of the roof, glue sheets of large drawing paper and the bottom of the plastic pencil case.

c. Cover one outside wall with a large chalkboard or two small chalkboards.

d. Cover the other outside wall with a white board.

e. On the back of the doghouse, glue on puzzles secured in boards.

More Ideas

Fill the doghouse with stuffed animals and keep it in a play corner. Fill the pencil case with crayons, chalk, whiteboard markers, etc.

To make a doghouse, use 2" x 4"s (5cm x 10cm) to make the floor, walls and roof base. Each 2" x 4" should be cut to 3' (90cm) long. Nail two 2" x 4"s together at a 90° angle. Do the same with two more 2" x 4"s. Join the two, to make a rectangle. Nail another 2" x 4" in the middle, to make the wall sturdier. Make six of these for the walls, floor and roof. Nail the three walls to the floor. Attach the roof with joists to the walls. Cover everything with quarter-inch plywood.

Kitten Kite

Kitten Kite

Materials

- Old nylon pants or nylon material
- Scissors
- Sewing machine and thread
- Permanent marker
- Two sticks, one that is slightly longer than the other
- Rope
- Packing tape

Preparation

a. Cut four equal-sized squares out of the old nylon pants and two small triangles.

b. Sew the squares together to make a larger square; or when turned, they make a large diamond.

c. Sew the two small triangles on each side of the peak of the top of the diamond. These will form the ears of the kitten.

Let's Do It

a. Place the smaller stick across the larger one, a small distance from the top, to form a "t."

b. Tie the sticks together in the middle without cutting the end off the rope.

c. Tape the top peak of the nylon diamond to the top of the t-shaped sticks.

d. Tape the rest of the kite to the sticks with the packing tape.

e. On the front of the kite, use the permanent marker to draw eyes, a kitten nose, and whiskers.

f. Try flying the kite outside, or use it to decorate a wall.

More Ideas

Kites can also be made from straws and garbage bags. Cut a large diamond from the plastic garbage bag and tape it to two straws taped or tied together in a t-shape.

Acrylic paint can also be used to make the face of the kitten on the kite.

You're a Monkey

134

You're a Monkey

Materials

- Large, plain beach towel
- Fabric paint
- Black permanent marker

Preparation

a. Wash and dry beach towel.

b. Read directions on the fabric paint thoroughly before beginning.

Let's Do It

a. Spread out beach towel on the floor and lay down in the center of it.

b. Bend your knees and point your toes out.

c. Bend your elbows and place any fly away hair behind your head.

d. Have someone outline your body, extending your arm outline to reach your knees.

e. Paint your outline with the face and fur of a monkey.

f. Allow the paint to dry before using.

More Ideas

Use a large sheet of paper and crayons, markers, or paint to make the monkey outline.

Hold a banana or a bunch of bananas in your hand as someone traces around you. Then include a jungle scene background behind and around the monkey outline.

A Bear-y Special Card

You are...

Bear-y Special to Me!

A Bear-y Special Card

Materials

- Thick paper in your color choice, cardstock works well
- Brown or black faux fur
- Scissors
- Glue
- Ribbon
- Two wiggle eyes
- Red felt
- Crayons or markers

Let's Do It

a. Fold the paper in half.

b. Cut out a bear figure from the faux fur.

c. Trace the bear figure on the front of the card paper and cut it out.

d. Glue the bear to the inside of the card. It should match up to the shape cut out of the front.

e. Decorate the bear with wiggle eyes, ribbon around the neck, and a red felt heart in the middle of the chest.

f. On the outside of the card, print the words "You are ..." and finish it on the inside by printing "Bear-y Special to Me!"

More Ideas

Make a book with the bear on the last page and a bear shape cut out of each page so that the bear can be seen on every page. Change the scene around the bear on each page.

Use this card as a Valentine card and give it to someone special.

Lion Head

Lion Head

Materials

- Brown powder tempera paint
- Yellow construction paper
- Brown marker
- Quilt batting
- Scissors
- Glue stick

Let's Do It

a. Sprinkle the brown powder tempera paint onto the quilt batting until it is fully covered with the brown paint.

b. Allow time for the paint to set and then shake any excess powder off of the batting into the garbage.

c. On the yellow construction paper, draw a large circle and two semi-circles on top of the circle for ears, with the brown marker.

d. Draw a face on the lion.

e. Glue the batting all the way around the circle head.

f. Cut out the picture around the batting used for the mane.

More Ideas

Make the whole lion by using more yellow construction paper to make the rest of the body and more batting for the end of the tail.

Make a large card by folding poster board in half and creating the lion out of batting. Print a catchy phrase on the inside such as:

"No Lion, you're great!"

or

"You're something to roar about!"

Fish Aquarium

Fish Aquarium

Materials

- Medium-sized box
- Blue paint and paintbrush
- White paper
- Small, white garbage bag
- String
- Rocks
- Scissors
- Tape
- Newspaper

Let's Do It

a. Paint the inside of the box blue and allow it to dry completely.

b. Cut fish shapes out of the white paper, two of each shape.

c. Stuff each fish with small bits of crumpled-up newspaper and tape around the edges to hold it together.

d. Stuff the bottom of a white garbage bag with crumpled-up newspaper and tape the middle of it together. This makes an octopus head. Cut eight strips from the bottom of the garbage bag to make the tentacles.

e. Make a small treasure chest and boat from white paper by folding it and bending the corners together. Tape where needed.

f. Place everything inside the box, attaching it with tape or string.

g. Add small rocks to the bottom to create the illusion of an aquarium.

More Ideas

Make a papier mâché octopus by stuffing an old pair of panty hose and then adding more panty hose legs to make the eight tentacles. Cover with papier mâché paste and newspaper. Paint the octopus when it's dry.

Create large, stuffed fish by cutting two equal-sized fish shapes from two pieces of poster board. Stuff them with newspaper and staple or tape them together as needed. Paint the fish to add color.

Pet Portraits

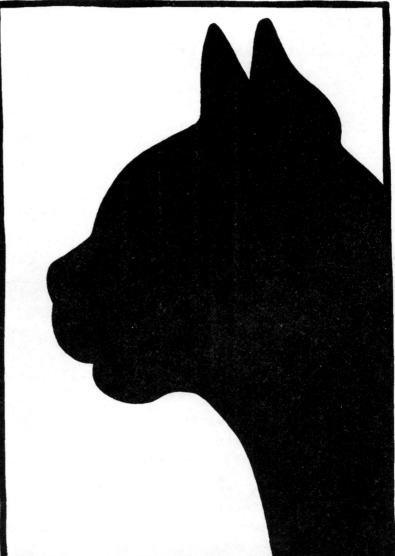

Pet Portraits

Materials

- Black construction paper
- White 11" x 14" paper
- Flashlight
- White chalk
- Tape
- Your favorite dog, cat, or fish
- Scissors
- Glue

Let's Do It

a. Tape a sheet of black construction paper on the wall and position your pet 2' (72 cm) in front of it.

b. About 4'–5' (1.2–1.5 m) in front of the black construction paper, position the flashlight and shine it at the construction paper.

c. Using white chalk, outline your pet's frame on the black construction paper.

d. Cut the silhouette out and glue it to the center of the white paper.

More Ideas

If you have trouble getting your pet to stay still, have someone pose with your pet, to keep your pet more content.

Frame your pet's portrait and hang it up for all to see.

Use a stuffed animal to create a silhouette.

Edible Animal Zoo

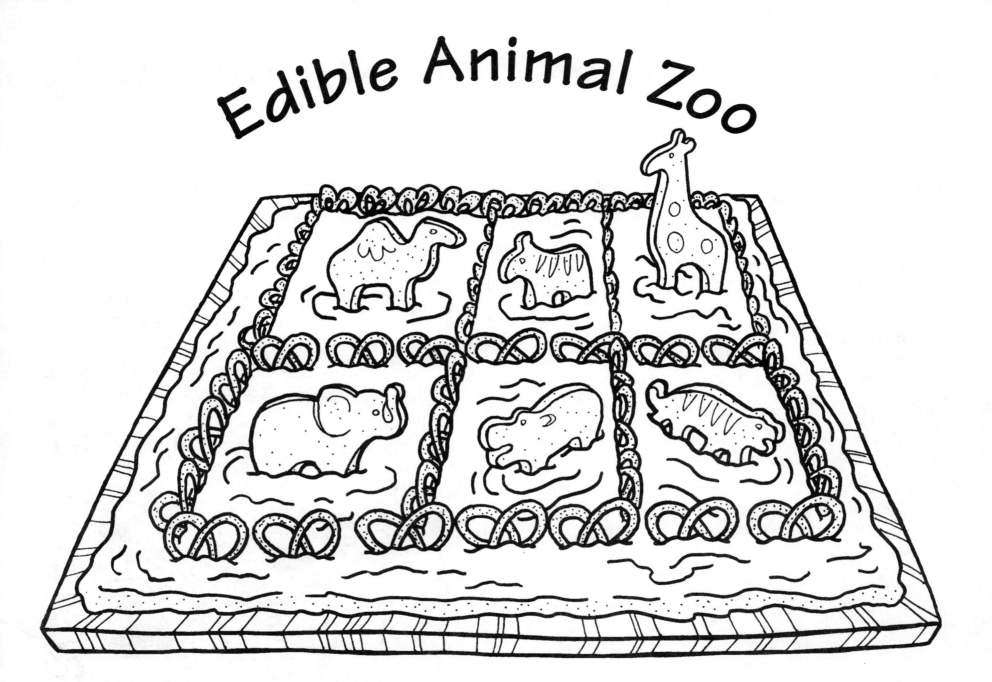

Edible Animal Zoo

Materials

- Cardboard
- Tinfoil
- Powdered sugar
- Water
- Bowl
- Spoon
- Pretzels
- Animal crackers

Let's Do It

a. Cover a small square of cardboard in tinfoil for the base of the zoo.

b. Mix three parts powdered sugar with one part water in a small bowl until you have a thick paste-like consistancy.

c. Spread the icing sugar paste onto the tinfoil and place pretzels into it, so they stand up, holding the first few until the paste starts to harden. The pretzels form the animal's cages.

d. Build cages from the pretzels and icing and allow time for it to dry and become hard.

e. In the middle of each pretzel cage, put a small amount of the icing and place an animal cracker in it.

More Ideas

Make your own animal cookies with different animal cookie cutters and your favorite shortbread recipe. Place these cookies in the cages.

To make your edible animal zoo as big or as small as you would like, make as many cages as you want with the pretzels and paste.

Use gummy animals instead of animal crackers for your zoo animals.

Use graham crackers to make houses for the animals.

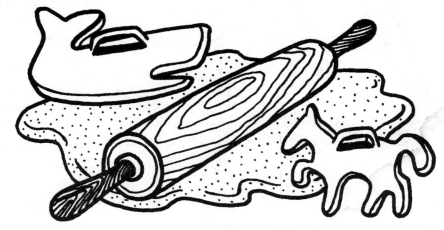

Reindeer Clothes

146

Reindeer Clothes

Materials

- Small piece of cardboard
- Pencil
- Scissors
- Brown paint and paintbrush
- Old ball cap
- Clear tape
- Brown pants
- Brown shirt
- White quilt batting
- Glue

Let's Do It

a. Use a pencil to draw antlers onto the cardboard and paint them brown. Allow time for it to dry.

b. Using scissors, cut the antlers out.

c. Tape the antlers to the back of a ball cap. Tape the middle of the antlers to the section where the hat can be adjusted. Go over it with tape, three or four times, so it holds well.

d. Glue a large, oval shape of quilt batting onto the front of the brown shirt.

e. Glue a small quilt batting tail to the seat of the brown pants.

More Ideas

To make a Rudolph the Red Nosed Reindeer costume, use face paint or a clown's nose to make a red nose. Wear bells around your neck to help guide Santa's sleigh.

If you don't have a brown shirt, take a plain white shirt and use brown fabric dye to color it.

Photography Frolics

Materials

- Black construction paper
- Tissue paper
- Scissors
- Glue
- Flashlight
- Plain sheet
- Tape
- Camera

Let's Do It

a. Cut a night sky scene out of black construction paper. Star, bird, or bat shapes are some ideas you could use.

b. Glue tissue paper to the back of the black paper so that the stars and birds are covered.

c. Tape a sheet to the wall and keep the room dark.

d. Shine a flashlight onto the sheet on the wall, placing your night sky picture in the middle. Your night scene will then be transferred to the sheet. You may need to ask an adult to help you.

e. Take a picture of the night sky you have portrayed on the sheet and have it developed.

f. Crop your photograph so that only the night sky is showing.

g. Show off your photo of a beautiful and bright night sky with birds or bats showing clearly in the photo.

More Ideas

Use your night sky scene and place it in a window so that the tissue paper catches the sunlight.

Create a Halloween night scene by cutting a moon and flying witch on the black construction paper. Cut out bats and black cats. Cover the back with yellow tissue paper.

Friendship Horse Cover

Friendship Horse Cover

Materials

- Large bed sheet
- Scissors
- Fabric paint
- Small thick blanket
- Fabric glue
- Old shower curtain with tassels, or tassels by the yard

Let's Do It

a. Cut equal-sized squares out of the large bed sheet.

b. Give each of your friends or family members a square and use fabric paint to decorate their name and something they like or enjoy.

c. When all of the squares are decorated and dry, glue them onto a blanket.

d. Glue the tassels from an old shower curtain along the edges.

e. Cover your favorite horse, pony, or bed with the blanket.

More Ideas

Make an animal quilt by cutting squares from a large bed sheet. Use fabric paint to decorate each square with a different animal. Glue or sew the squares together. Decorate with tassels and trim.

Sew hooks on the top of the blanket and hang your quilt to display it.

If a sewing machine is available, sew everything together instead of using fabric glue.

Make a smaller quilt to welcome a new baby brother or sister into the family.

Penguin Soap

Penguin Soap

Materials

- Bowl
- Black food coloring (available at craft or cake decorating stores)
- Soap flakes
- Water
- Ribbon
- Cake decorating balls
- Thin metal wire

Let's Do It

a. Measure one and a half cups of soap flakes and pour them into the bowl.

b. Mix in two tablespoons of water and two drops of black food coloring into the soap flakes.

c. Shape the soap flakes into two balls, one larger than the other.

d. When the balls are firm, use a small piece of wire to connect them so they look like a head and a body.

e. Mix a quarter of a cup of soap flakes and one teaspoon of water in the bowl and make two flat pancake-shaped circles. Press them onto the head and body of the black soap. This makes the white part of the penguin body.

f. Press the cake-decorating balls into the soap to make the eyes and tie a ribbon around the neck to finish the decorating.

More Ideas

Add a small scarf to decorate the penguin.

Make other animals out of the soap flakes by just changing the food coloring and the shape of the soap.

Press the soap mixture flat and use cookie cutters to make shapes. You could even string them on a rope before they dry so you can hang them in the shower.

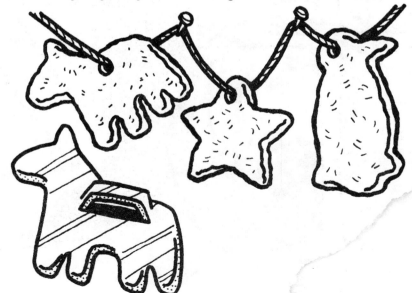

"Elevent" Nose

"Elevent" Nose

Materials

- Dryer venting
- Gray or silver spray paint
- Single hole puncher
- Sewing elastic
- Stapler
- Pink construction paper

Let's Do It

a. Spray paint the dryer venting gray or silver. Allow time for it to dry completely.

b. Punch two holes at the top of the dryer venting, one on each side.

c. Tie the elastic through the holes, making it snug around your nose and head.

d. Cut out a horseshoe shape from the pink construction paper.

e. Staple the construction paper to the inside of the venting at the opposite end of the elastic.

More Ideas

Make elephant ears to go with the "elevent" nose. Cut elephant ear shapes out of plastic milk jugs. Paint the ears with gray acrylic paint.

Make a cardboard box elephant with a medium-sized cardboard box painted gray. Glue three, large paper plates side-by-side on the outside of the box to make the face and ears. Attach the dryer venting nose. Make legs from four milk cartons. You could also cut a large hole in the top of the box for your body and two large holes in the bottom of the box for your legs. Get inside the box and pretend to be an elephant. You could use your costume for Halloween.

Dress up as an elephant and pretend to be an elephant marching through the jungle.

Yellow Duck

Yellow Duck

Materials

- Flowing yellow dress or extra large yellow T-shirt
- Medium-sized box
- Black marker or fabric paint
- Orange construction paper
- Sewing elastic
- Single hole punch
- Glue
- Tape

Let's Do It

a. Open the box on both ends so that you can pull the box up around your body.

b. Place the yellow dress or T-shirt over the top opening of the box and glue it in place. You should be able to put the box over your head and put the arms in the armholes of the shirt or dress and your head through the neck hole.

c. Use black marker or paint to draw wings on the sides of the box.

d. Make a cone shape out of orange construction paper and secure with tape.

e. To make the beak, punch a hole on each side of the large opening of the cone shape and tie elastic through the holes to fit snug around your head.

More Ideas

Complete the outfit with a yellow hat. If you don't have a yellow hat, use an old hat and paint it yellow with fabric paint.

Make a yellow bulldozer by gluing a yellow dress or T-shirt over a box. Draw tires on each side of the box instead of wings. Make a loader from a large box by cutting one side off of the box, with two cardboard arms stapled to the edges of the box. Hold each arm with your hands to lift the loader up and down.

Farmyard Fun

Farmyard Fun

Materials

- Round straw or hay bales
- Tractor with forks and an operator
- Paper
- Pencil

Let's Do It

a. Draw an outline for a maze made of bales on paper.

b. Have an operator use the tractor to move round bales to follow the outline you have created.

c. Make sure the opening between the bales is wide enough to walk through.

d. Never stack round bales on top of each other.

More Ideas

Square bales can be used to make the maze, as long as they are kept in stacks.

If bales and space are unavailable, use stacked boxes to create a large walk-through maze.

Index